**Harvard
Business
Review**

on

REBUILDING YOUR BUSINESS MODEL

D0684491

The Harvard Business Review
Paperback series

If you need the best practices and ideas for the business challenges you face—but don't have time to find them—***Harvard Business Review* paperbacks** are for you. Each book is a collection of HBR's inspiring and useful perspectives on a given management topic, all in one place.

The titles include:

Harvard Business Review

on

REBUILDING YOUR BUSINESS MODEL

Harvard Business Review Press

Boston, Massachusetts

Copyright 2011 Harvard Business School Publishing Corporation

All rights reserved

Printed in the United States of America

10 9 8 7 6 5 4 3 2 1

No part of this publication may be reproduced, stored in or introduced into a retrieval system, or transmitted, in any form, or by any means (electronic, mechanical, photocopying, recording, or otherwise), without the prior permission of the publisher. Requests for permission should be directed to permissions@hbsp.harvard.edu, or mailed to Permissions, Harvard Business School Publishing, 60 Harvard Way, Boston, Massachusetts 02163.

Library of Congress Cataloging-in-Publication Data

Harvard business review on rebuilding your business model.
    p. cm.—(The Harvard business review paperback series)
    ISBN 978-1-4221-6262-0 (alk. paper)
    1. Business planning. 2. Strategic planning. I. Harvard business review.
    HD30.28.H3793   2011
    658.4'012—dc22

                                                  2011007228

Contents

**Harvard
Business
Review**

on

REBUILDING YOUR BUSINESS MODEL

The CEO's Role In Business Model Reinvention

A forward-looking CEO must do three things: Manage the present, selectively forget the past, and create the future.

by Vijay Govindarajan and Chris Trimble

CONSIDER A FEW of the great innovation stories of the past decade: Google, Netflix, and Skype. Now ask yourself, why wasn't Google created by Microsoft? Netflix by Blockbuster? Skype by AT&T?

Why do established corporations struggle to find the next big thing before new competitors do? The problem is pervasive; the examples are countless. The simple explanation is that many companies become too focused on executing today's business model and forget that business models are perishable. Success today does not guarantee success tomorrow.

To assess your company's vulnerability, try this diagnostic: On separate index cards, write down all the important initiatives under way in your organization. Then create three boxes and label them "Box 1: Manage the Present," "Box 2: Selectively Forget the Past," and "Box 3: Create the Future."

Next, take a few minutes to imagine your industry in five, 10, or even 20 years—as far out as you can reasonably foresee. Consider all the forces of change your industry faces—technology, customer demographics, regulation, globalization, and so on. With those forces in mind, put your organization's initiatives in the appropriate boxes: those intended to improve today's business performance in box 1; those aimed at stopping something—underperforming products and services, obsolete policies and practices, outdated assumptions and mind-sets—in box 2; and those that prepare your organization for the long term in box 3.

For companies to endure, they must get the forces of preservation (box 1), destruction (box 2), and creation (box 3) in the right balance. Striking that balance is the CEO's most important task, but most companies overwhelmingly favor box 1. Forces of preservation reign supreme. Forces of destruction and creation are overshadowed, outmatched, and out of luck.

To be sure, the work of preservation—the day-to-day execution of the existing business model—is vitally important. CEOs must get box 1 right or their tenures will be short. They must concentrate daily on performance excellence and continuous improvement, as companies such as Wal-Mart and Southwest Airlines have done for years. The best box 1 companies are sleek and efficient, like a well-designed

Idea in Brief

Forward-looking CEOs must harness the power of the past, the present, and the future in three critical disciplines.

	Box 1 Manage the present	Box 2 Selectively forget the past	Box 3 Create the future
	You are accustomed to	You must recognize that	So that you can
Strategy making	Data-driven analysis	Rich data about the future are not available. The best you can do is to consider long-term trends and potential nonlinear shifts.	Create a separate, parallel strategy-making process for box 3. Involve nontraditional voices.
Accountability	Strict accountability for results	The alternative to accountability for results is not anarchy. It is a different kind of accountability.	Hold leaders of box 3 projects accountable for running disciplined experiments.
Organizational design	Perfect alignment	An organization that is perfectly aligned can operate only in box 1.	Create zero-based, custom-built subunits for box 3 projects.

automobile. They coordinate an astonishingly complex array of human actions like so many gears, pistons, and camshafts.

But CEOs are not *just* responsible for box 1. They must also get boxes 2 and 3 right. Sadly, most chief executives ignore destruction and creation until it is too late. They bow to a myriad of short-term pressures: intense demands for quarterly earnings, risk aversion, discomfort with uncertainty, resistance to change, linear extrapolation from past experience, and unwillingness to cannibalize established businesses. As a result, many companies fail to transform themselves.

The failure may not be immediately apparent, but sooner or later most industries go through nonlinear shifts that threaten incumbents. For instance, breakthroughs in genetic engineering have revolutionized the pharmaceutical industry. New concerns about environmental quality have posed serious threats in energy-intensive sectors. Globalization has opened up India and China, where unfamiliar rivals are challenging established companies with ultra-low-price products.

While most companies neatly manage linear change, they are left befuddled by nonlinear change. Transformation efforts look meek at best, like futilely trying to turn a car into an airplane by bolting on two wings. Consider, for example, Sony's lagging positions in portable music players and electronic book readers, or Nokia's and Motorola's struggles to keep up with the rapid evolution of smartphones.

To win both today and tomorrow, CEOs must operate in all three boxes simultaneously. They must recognize that boxes 2 and 3 are not about what the business will be doing in 20 years; they are about the preparations it must make today. That's easier said than done, for it's not only a matter of balancing resources across the three boxes. The CEO must also know exactly what to destroy and what to create.

On the surface, box 2 is about pruning lines of business that are underperforming or no longer fit the company's strategy. Some companies do that consistently. For decades, for example, Corning has been eliminating mature businesses, such as cookware and light bulbs, to focus on high-growth opportunities. And when Japanese firms commoditized the market for dynamic random-access memory—a key component in PCs— Intel cofounder Andy Grove shifted the company into microprocessors. Such divestitures are traumatic but not conceptually mysterious. Pruning simply requires commitment from powerful executives.

It's harder to take a knife to a less-evident box 2 menace: organizational memory. As managers run the core business, they develop biases, assumptions, and entrenched mind-sets. These become further embedded in planning processes, performance evaluation systems, organizational structures, and human resources policies. Organizational memory is particularly powerful in companies that tend to promote from within and to have homogeneous cultures, strong socialization mechanisms, and long track records of success. Such deeply rooted memory may be great for preservation (box 1), but if it is not tamed sufficiently (box 2), it gets in the way of creation (box 3). That's why all box 3 initiatives must start in box 2. Bottom line: Before you can create, you must forget.

To understand how a company can manage all three boxes successfully, let's look at Infosys Technologies Limited of India.

Business Model Transformation at Infosys

On July 31, 2006, Infosys chairman N.R. Narayana Murthy stood before thousands of employees in Mysore, India, and pressed an orange button. Half a world away, trading commenced on the Nasdaq. His remotely ringing the opening bell, part of Infosys's 25-year anniversary celebration, symbolized how the global economy was being transformed.

For people trying to understand the offshoring phenomenon, Infosys was exhibit A. Indeed, it had inspired Thomas Friedman to write *The World Is Flat*. The company had demonstrated that its core service, custom software development for corporations, did not have to happen at the client site. Most of the work could be done thousands of miles away in talent-rich but low-cost India. Infosys dubbed its approach the "global delivery model."

Infosys's rapid rise is legendary in India. In the 1980s the company was just a small group of programmers who had traveled from South Asia to the United States to offer their services. But in the early 1990s India's rapid deregulation and the rise of the internet opened the door for the global delivery model. Today Infosys is a $5 billion IT services firm with more than 100,000 employees and a market cap of nearly $40 billion.

During the late 1990s, with revenues growing rapidly, Infosys could easily have focused on preservation. But Murthy was intent on challenging the biggest companies in the IT services industry, including IBM and Accenture. He and then-CEO Nandan Nilekani had a hypothesis about how the industry would evolve. The company's most demanding clients were frustrated by having to work simultaneously with multiple services firms, each lacking full accountability. Eventually, Murthy and Nilekani believed, clients would hire just one firm that could deliver end-to-end IT services. The hypothetical company would provide a management consulting team that would redesign operations and write specifications for new IT systems. That same company would then develop, test, install, and maintain the new hardware and software—and might even accept responsibility for executing routine client operations such as transaction processing.

This implied a dramatic industry transformation. If multiple rivals moved toward end-to-end services, former partners would become rivals. The industry would have room for only a handful of very large players. Infosys intended to be one of them—and to use its mastery of the global delivery model to outperform rivals. To accomplish that, the company needed to create several new services even as it continued executing its existing, fast-growing business. By pushing into boxes 2 and 3, Infosys grew 25-fold, from $200 million to $5 billion in the past decade. Revenues from services other than its original offering—custom software development—grew from a small base in the 1990s, to 40% by 2003, and to nearly 60% by 2010.

Infosys succeeded in avoiding the box 2 hazard of organizational memory. By building a parallel "box 2/3" world with different people and distinct processes, it was able to create the future while sustaining excellence in box 1. In the process, Infosys paid especially close attention to three critical disciplines: strategy making, accountability, and organizational design.

Strategy Making

The central tenets of strategy making are well known. It should be an analytical, data-driven process that rigorously identifies customer needs, differentiates the company from rivals, and maximizes profits. But despite its many merits, this process also systematically squeezes out box 3 thinking. Leaders who insist on rigorously analyzed data tend to resist making change on the basis of limited evidence or weak signals. The result: a short-term mind-set; a strict focus on existing customers, not emerging ones; an obsession with today's rivals, not potential entrants; an emphasis on leveraging existing competencies rather than building new ones; and a tacit assumption that lines of demarcation between markets are fixed.

Box 3 strategy making is very different. Endeavors of creation must begin with a destructive (box 2) action—abandoning traditional strategy practices in favor of new ones. Box 3 strategy is not about linear extrapolation from the past; it's about trying to anticipate nonlinear shifts. That's a tough—but necessary—concept to grasp if you're a senior leader who rose to the top of an organization by excelling in box 1.

Infosys smartly brought nontraditional voices into the box 3 strategy process. For example, it directly engaged a subset of its clients, in group and one-on-one meetings, to challenge the company's long-range assumptions and to make provocative suggestions for future growth. As a direct result of this interaction, Infosys chose to redouble its investment in an experimental business unit that offered packaged software for Indian bank branches—and to adapt it for worldwide use.

Infosys relied even more heavily on input from young employees. It assembled a Voices of Youth panel of high performers who participated annually in eight senior management meetings. In putting together this team, Murthy cited what he calls the "30/30 rule": 30% of participants in any strategy discussion should be younger than age 30, because they are creative and not wedded to the past. In addition, Infosys created several inventive and colorfully named mechanisms—strategy graffiti walls, knowledge cafés, jam sessions, and speed-geeking—to continually attract thousands of young employees to the process. Jam sessions, for instance, are fast-paced round-table meetings in which each participant has just one minute to give an impromptu response to questions such as "How can Infosys win in emerging markets?" The company even developed software that automated the process of sifting through huge volumes of responses, to identify common themes and unique ideas. Murthy credits youth involvement for sparking more than 10 R&D projects at Infosys, on topics ranging from health care to sustainability to education.

Accountability

To succeed at preservation (box 1), successful companies develop mechanisms that hold individuals accountable for results. Those who deliver on time, on budget, and on spec should earn raises and promotions; those who don't are probably better suited for other careers. Companies with demanding performance cultures, such as GE, tend to do very well in box 1. But, again, initiatives to create the future must begin by forgetting the past. Strict accountability for results must be left behind to allow for conjectures about potential nonlinear shifts. Those conjectures are best tested by running disciplined experiments.

For example, in 1999 IBM launched an effort to multiply computing speeds by a factor of 500. IBM's conjecture was that the next generation of supercomputers would not run on one super-fast chip but on huge networks of ordinary chips. IBM's machine, dubbed Blue-Gene, would, as imagined, run massive simulations for scientists who study climate change, particle physics, cellular processes, and more. The big unknown, however, was the relationship between the number of chips and the volume of communications among them. It was possible that the network that tied the chips together would clog up like Los Angeles freeways at rush hour. To pinpoint when that would happen, IBM developed a systematic test plan. It first built a prototype with just two chips, then four, then eight. It ran disciplined experiments with each prototype. If BlueGene were to fail, IBM would learn at the lowest cost possible. By 2007 the company had succeeded in building a 212,992-chip Blue-Gene, the fastest supercomputer in the world.

When leaders of box 3 initiatives learn fast (and at minimal cost), they make better decisions. They either find success or exit quickly and cheaply. But disciplined experimentation is not easy. As we describe in our book *The Other Side of Innovation*, best practices for planning experiments look almost nothing like best practices for ongoing operations. Therefore, it's critical to use distinct methods to evaluate the results of box 3 initiatives and the performance of their leaders.

Consider the negative consequences of subjecting a leader to a traditional, results-focused performance assessment while she operates in box 3. Uncertainties are high, and assumptions often prove wrong, yielding disappointing results and leaders who get defensive about them. Open discussion disappears, learning ceases, and bad decision making tends to ensue. Instead, leaders should be held accountable for learning quickly from disciplined experiments that they conduct in box 3. Administered properly, this form of accountability is anything but forgiving. It requires intense reasoning and ruthless analysis of assumptions.

Infosys has developed a very strong culture of accountability for results. In fact, it created an acronym for its expectations of business unit leaders' actions— namely, that they be predictable, sustainable, profitable, and de-risked: PSPD. Still, Infosys maintains different kinds of expectations for new services—standards that allow for greater uncertainty but are no less forgiving.

In 2002 Infosys launched a fundamentally new (box 3) business for the company: Infosys Consulting. Instead of producing custom software, the new consulting unit would advise clients on redesigning their operations; rather than calling on heads of IT, it would serve general managers. The core business of software programming was almost a science, whereas Infosys Consulting was more of an art.

Murthy and Nilekani knew it was unrealistic to expect its new service to immediately deliver predictable, sustainable, profitable, and de-risked results. So they exempted it from traditional performance review forums and had it report to an internal board of directors. That board looked for clear signs that Infosys Consulting was headed toward success. For example, it expected an upward trend in per-employee revenues as time dedicated to selling services declined and time dedicated to delivering services rose. The board also altered expectations about forecast accuracy for Infosys Consulting: not 99%, as required of established units, but 50%, at least at first. As the team learned, its forecasts naturally improved.

Organizational Design

To achieve day-to-day excellence (box 1), companies must do more than hire and train outstanding individuals. They must optimize the way individuals collaborate—through job specifications, organizational designs, and work processes. When all individuals are perfectly aligned, companies become works of high art. However, a box 1 work of art is also a highly specialized machine. As such, it's unrealistic to expect to be able to just "squeeze in" a box 3 project. Special teams are essential. The first step in building them is a box 2 action—dropping standard organizational practices. Box 3 projects require zero-based, custom-built subunits.

Forming these subunits is an act of creation even more significant than generating a breakthrough box 3 idea. As we explained in "Stop the Innovation Wars" (HBR July–August 2010), it's much like building a new company from scratch. Outsiders play a critical role by bringing in new skills and catalyzing change. They are powerful box 2 agents because they naturally challenge assumptions.

Infosys Consulting was a box 3 project, so Murthy and Nilekani created a new, distinct subunit. They hired an outsider with 15 years of consulting experience to lead the effort, and they lured several more senior partners from other consulting firms. Then, rather than creating a unit based on Infosys's existing organizational structure, they studied other firms' processes and organizational designs and altered them for the global delivery model. Today Infosys Consulting generates more than $100 million in revenues annually.

That's a much more favorable outcome than what happened when one of the Big Three U.S. automakers first entered India in the early 1990s. The tremendous economic divide between India and the United States demanded a box 3 approach to making an automobile. Rather than creating a zero-based subunit in India to

The High Jump "Industry"

The history of the Olympic high jump event illustrates the importance of adapting to nonlinear change. It has evolved through four distinct "business models."

Early on, the "scissors" style dominated the sport. It was much like hurdling. All high jumpers used the scissors approach, so winning meant being the best at it. The high jumpers were operating in box 1 (preservation). Had they been businesspeople, they would have been competing on cost, market share, and margins.

High jumpers remained in box 1 at their peril, however. Even the best athletes could improve upon the established technique only incrementally. The approach had severe limitations because the jumper's center of gravity had to rise much higher than the bar.

More-innovative jumpers broke the high jump down into two fundamentals: raising one's center of gravity (jumping higher) and raising it no more than necessary to clear the bar (avoiding "wasted lift"). It turned out that although finding ways to jump higher was quite difficult, athletes could find plenty of opportunities to avoid wasted lift. High jumpers created three new styles.

First, they invented the "western roll," in which jumpers launched and landed on the same foot and kept their backs to the bar. Then they discovered the "straddle," in which they launched and landed on opposite feet and faced the bar. Finally, in the 1968 Olympics,

---

spearhead the effort, however, the company engineered the car in Detroit and, to cut costs, decided to put power windows only in the front doors. That decision initially seemed reasonable, but at that time any Indian who could afford a car could also afford a chauffeur. The owner, sitting in the back, had to use hand-crank windows. It's one reason why this U.S. automaker

Dick Fosbury created the surprising Fosbury Flop, which required twisting 180 degrees and landing on one's head. To succeed, Fosbury had to unlearn everything his coaches had taught him about speed, angle of approach, and technique.

Each new jumping style transformed the high jump "industry." The innovators had to somehow forget best practices (box 2) and create next practices (box 3). Many other jumpers, trapped by the forces of preservation (box 1), failed to remain competitive.

Olympic gold medal winners in high jump

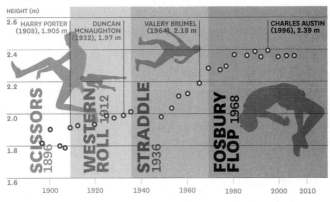

Olympic games were not held in 1916, 1940, and 1944.

is still largely irrelevant in one of the world's fastest-growing automotive markets.

Prioritizing for the Long Term

As we have discussed, the secret to winning over the long run lies in knowing what to forget and what to

The Transformation Process
in Hindu Mythology

HINDUISM PROVIDES A UNIQUE window into the three perspectives we focus on in this article: managing the present, selectively forgetting the past, and creating the future. The religion recognizes many gods but only three main deities: Vishnu, the god of preservation (box 1); Shiva, the god of destruction (box 2); and Brahma, the god of creation (box 3).

The Hindu mythmakers even paired each of the three gods with symbolically relevant wives. Vishnu was married to Lakshmi, who bestowed wealth—just as box 1 produces current income. Shiva's partner was Parvathi, who symbolized power, a vital box 2 necessity when selectively destroying the past. Brahma was betrothed to Saraswathi, who symbolized creativity, ideas, and knowledge—critical inputs in formulating box 3 strategies.

According to Hindu philosophy, the balanced interactions among the three gods create a continuous preservation–destruction–creation cycle that helps sustain all forms of life in a circle without a beginning or an end. Achieving that continuous cycle is a goal worthy of any farsighted organization.

---

create. Still, every box 3 initiative requires a tough first step: making the commitment to launch. Shifting resources from the present to the future may be the most difficult challenge for CEOs, given the enormous short-term pressures they face routinely.

In its early days, Infosys had a *Fortune* 10 client that accounted for 25% of its revenues and was demanding substantial price concessions. Murthy walked away and accepted a devastating blow to short-term performance. His simple rationale: Infosys would never agree to a price so low that it would have to sacrifice service quality or cut investments in people, training, R&D, and technology. Doing so, he reasoned, would damage the brand and undermine the company's future.

The most intense short-term pressures come not from clients, however, but from Wall Street, which demands reliable earnings growth and richly rewards CEOs who deliver it. This powerful box 1 incentive cripples the forces of destruction and creation because box 3 projects inevitably have a worse-before-better impact on the bottom line. Further, CEOs' tenures are short relative to the rhythm of transformation efforts. By the time box 3 projects pay off, many will have retired, so they are tempted to focus on the immediate and leave on a high note.

Murthy, by contrast, views Infosys as a lifelong endeavor. His approach to investors has been steadfast: Relentlessly promote long-term potential; immediately share short-term disappointment. Murthy volunteered the bad news of the loss of the major client to investors within 48 hours. Then he returned to finding the right balance among the forces of preservation, destruction, and creation. This balance is the secret to Infosys's mastery of both the present and the future, and it must be the foundation for any business institution that aspires to endure for generations.

VIJAY GOVINDARAJAN is the Earl C. Daum 1924 Professor of International Business and the founding director of the Center for Global Leadership at the Tuck School of Business at Dartmouth. He was General Electric's first professor in residence and chief innovation consultant. **CHRIS TRIMBLE** is on the faculty at Tuck and is an expert on innovation within established organizations. They are the authors of *The Other Side of Innovation: Solving the Execution Challenge* (Harvard Business Review Press, 2010).

Originally published in January 2011. Reprint R1101H

Reinvent Your Business Before It's Too Late

Watch Out for Those S Curves
by Paul Nunes and Tim Breene

SOONER OR LATER, all businesses, even the most successful, run out of room to grow. Faced with this unpleasant reality, they are compelled to reinvent themselves periodically. The ability to pull off this difficult feat—to jump from the maturity stage of one business to the growth stage of the next—is what separates high performers from those whose time at the top is all too brief.

The potential consequences are dire for any organization that fails to reinvent itself in time. As Matthew S. Olson and Derek van Bever demonstrate in their book *Stall Points,* once a company runs up against a major stall in its growth, it has less than a 10% chance of ever fully recovering. Those odds are certainly daunting, and they do much to explain why two-thirds of stalled companies are later acquired, taken private, or forced into bankruptcy.

There's no shortage of explanations for this stalling—from failure to stick with the core (or sticking with it for too long) to problems with execution, misreading of consumer tastes, or an unhealthy focus on scale for scale's sake. What those theories have in common is the notion that stalling results from a failure to fix what is clearly broken in a company.

Having spent the better part of a decade researching the nature of high performance in business, we realized that those explanations missed something crucial. Companies fail to reinvent themselves not necessarily

Jumping the S curve

High performers are well on their way to new-business success by the time their existing businesses start to stall.

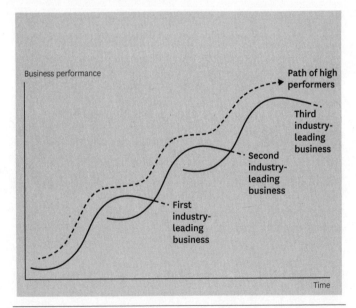

Idea in Brief

To survive over the long haul, a company must reinvent itself periodically, jumping from the flattening end of one business performance curve to the rising slope of another. Very few companies make the leap successfully when the time comes. That's because they start the reinvention process too late. Once existing business begins to stall and revenue growth drops significantly, a company has less than a 10% chance of ever fully recovering. Accenture's Nunes and Breene, reporting on the results of their long-running High Performance Business research program,

point to a striking difference between companies that have successfully reinvented themselves and those that failed. High performers manage their businesses not just along the growth curve of their revenues but also along three much shorter, though equally important, S curves: tracking the basis of competition in their industry, renewing their capabilities, and nurturing a ready supply of talent. By planting the seeds for new businesses before revenues from existing ones begin to stall, these companies enjoy sustained high performance.

because they are bad at fixing what's broken, but because they wait much too long before repairing the deteriorating bulwarks of the company. That is, they invest most of their energy managing to the contours of their existing operations—the financial S curve in which sales of a successful new offering build slowly, then ascend rapidly, and finally taper off—and not nearly enough energy creating the foundations of successful new businesses. Because of that, they are left scrambling when their core markets begin to stagnate.

In our research, we've found that the companies that successfully reinvent themselves have one trait in common. They tend to broaden their focus beyond the financial S curve and manage to three much shorter but vitally important hidden S curves—tracking the basis of competition in their industry, renewing their capabilities, and nurturing a ready supply of talent. In essence, they turn conventional wisdom on its head and learn to focus on fixing what doesn't yet appear to be broken.

Thrown a Curve

Making a commitment to reinvention before the need is glaringly obvious doesn't come naturally. Things often look rosiest just before a company heads into decline: Revenues from the current business model are surging, profits are robust, and the company stock commands a hefty premium. But that's exactly when managers need to take action.

To position themselves to jump to the next business S curve, they need to focus on the following.

The Hidden Competition Curve

Long before a successful business hits its revenue peak, the basis of competition on which it was founded expires. Competition in the cell phone industry, for instance, has changed several times—for both manufacturers and service providers—from price to network coverage to the value of services to design, branding, and applications. The first hidden S curve tracks how competition in an industry is shifting. High performers see changes in customer needs and create the next basis of competition in their industry, even as they exploit existing businesses that have not yet peaked.

Netflix, for example, radically altered the basis of competition in DVD rentals by introducing a business model that used delivery by mail. At the same time, it almost immediately set out to reinvent itself by capturing the technology that would replace physical copies of films—digital streaming over the internet. Today Netflix is the largest provider of DVDs by mail and a major player in online streaming. In contrast, Blockbuster rode its successful superstore model all the way to the top, tweaking it along the way (no more late fees) but failing to respond quickly enough to changes in the basis of competition.

The Hidden Capabilities Curve

In building the offerings that enable them to climb the financial S curve, high performers invariably create distinctive capabilities. Prominent examples include Dell with its direct model of PC sales, Wal-Mart with its unique supply chain capabilities, and Toyota with not just its production method but also its engineering capabilities, which made possible Lexus's luxury cars and the Prius. But distinctiveness in capabilities—like the basis of competition—is fleeting, so executives must invest in developing new ones in order to jump to the next capabilities S curve. All too often, though, the end of the capabilities curve does not become apparent to executives until time to develop a new one has run out.

Take the music industry. The major players concentrated on refining current operations; it was a PC maker that developed the capabilities needed to deliver digital music to millions of consumers at an acceptable price. High performers are continually looking for ways to reinvent themselves and their market. P&G long ago recognized the untapped customer market for disposable diapers. The company spent five years perfecting the capabilities that would allow diapers to be priced similarly to what customers were then paying services to launder and deliver cloth diapers. Amazon.com CEO Jeff Bezos notes that it takes five to seven years before the seeds his company plants—things like expanding beyond media products, working with third-party sellers, and going international—grow enough to have a meaningful impact on the economics of the business; this process requires foresight, early commitment, and tenacious faith in the power of R&D.

The Hidden Talent Curve

Companies often lose focus on developing and retaining enough of what we call serious talent—people with both the capabilities and the will to drive new business growth. This is especially true when the business is successfully humming along but has not yet peaked. In such circumstances, companies feel that operations can be leaner (they've moved far down the learning curve by then) and meaner, because they're under pressures to boost margins. They reduce both head count and investments in talent, which has the perverse effect of driving away the very people they could rely on to help them reinvent the business.

The high performers in our study maintain a steady commitment to talent creation. The oil-field services provider Schlumberger is always searching for and developing serious talent, assigning "ambassadors" to dozens of top engineering schools around the world.

These ambassadors include high-level executives who manage large budgets and can approve equipment donations and research funding at those universities. Close ties with the schools help Schlumberger get preference when it is recruiting. Not only does Schlumberger keep its talent pipeline flowing, but it's a leader in employee development. In fact, it is a net producer of talent for its industry, a hallmark of high performers.

By managing to these hidden curves—as well as keeping focused on the revenue growth S curve, it must be emphasized—the high performers in our study had typically started the reinvention process well before their current businesses had begun to slow. So what are the management practices that prepare high performers for reinvention? Let's look first at the response to the hidden competition curve.

Edge-Centric Strategy

Traditional strategic-planning methods are useful in stretching the revenue S curve of an existing business, but they can't help companies detect how the basis for competition in a market will change.

To make reinvention possible, companies must supplement their traditional approaches with a parallel strategy process that brings the edges of the market and the edges of the organization to the center. In this "edge-centric" approach, strategy making becomes a permanent activity without permanent structures or processes.

The Hidden S curves of high performance

Three aspects of a business mature—and start to decline—much faster than financial performance does. They need to be reinvented before you can grow a new business.

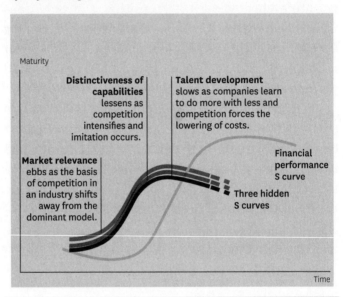

Maturity

Distinctiveness of capabilities lessens as competition intensifies and imitation occurs.

Talent development slows as companies learn to do more with less and competition forces the lowering of costs.

Market relevance ebbs as the basis of competition in an industry shifts away from the dominant model.

Financial performance S curve

Three hidden S curves

Time

Moving the Edge of the Market to the Center

An edge-centric strategy allows companies to continually scan the periphery of the market for untapped customer needs or unsolved problems. Consider how Novo Nordisk gets to the edge of the market to detect changes in the basis of competition as they're occurring. For example, through one critical initiative the pharma giant came to understand that its future businesses would have to address much more than physical health. The initiative—Diabetes Attitudes, Wishes, and Needs

(DAWN)—brings together thousands of primary care physicians, nurses, medical specialists, patients, and delegates from major associations like the World Health Organization to put the individual—rather than the disease—at the center of diabetes care.

Research conducted through DAWN has opened Novo's eyes to the psychological and sociological needs of patients. For example, the company learned that more than 40% of people with diabetes also have psychological issues, and about 15% suffer from depression. Because of such insights, the company has begun to reinvent itself early; it focuses less on drug development and manufacturing and more on disease prevention and treatment, betting that the future of the company lies in concentrating on the person as well as the disease.

Moving the Edge of the Organization to the Center

Frontline employees, far-flung research teams, line managers—all these individuals have a vital role to play in detecting important shifts in the market. High performers find ways to bring these voices into the strategy-making process. Best Buy listens to store managers far from corporate headquarters, such as the New York City manager who created a magnet store for Portuguese visitors coming off cruise ships. Reckitt Benckiser got one of its most successful product ideas, Air Wick Freshmatic, from a brand manager in Korea. The idea was initially met with considerable internal skepticism because it would require the company to incorporate electronics for the first time—but CEO Bart Becht is more impressed by passion than by consensus.

If strategy making is to remain on the edge, it cannot be formalized. We found that although low and average performers tend to make strategy according to the calendar, high performers use many methods and keep the timing dynamic to avoid predictability and to prevent the system from being gamed.

As quickly as competition shifts, the distinctiveness of capabilities may evaporate even faster. By the time a business really takes off, imitators have usually had time to plan and begin their attack, and others, attracted to marketplace success, are sure to follow. How, then, do companies build the capabilities necessary to jump to a new financial S curve?

Change at the Top

Some executives excel at running a business—ramping up manufacturing, expanding into different geographies, or extending a product line. Others are entrepreneurial—their strength is in creating new markets. Neither is inherently better; what matters is that the capabilities of the top team match the firm's organizational needs on the capabilities S curve. Companies run into trouble when their top teams stay in place to manage the financial S curve rather than evolve to build the next set of distinctive capabilities.

Avoiding that trap runs counter to human nature, of course. What member of a top team wants to leave when business is good? High performers recognize that a key to building the capabilities necessary to jump to a new financial S curve is the early injection

About the Research

AT ACCENTURE, WE HAVE BEEN conducting the High Performance Business research program since 2003. Starting from the premise that all performance is relative, we examined sets of peer companies. Previous research on high performance had compared companies head-to-head across industries, but that approach ignored the differences in average profitability, maturity, and risk from one industry to another, making it a contest among industries rather than among companies.

We settled on 31 peer sets for our initial study, encompassing more than 800 companies and representing more than 80% of the market capitalization of the Russell 3000 Index at the time. We analyzed performance in terms of 13 financial metrics to assess growth, profitability, consistency, longevity, and positioning for the future. In most cases, we applied the metrics over a 10-year span.

The businesses that performed extraordinarily well over the long term had all made regular transitions from maturing markets to new, vibrant ones. To find out how these organizations were able to maintain a high level of performance, we conducted years of follow-on investigation, creating special teams from our industry and business-function practice areas. Team members' expertise and experience was supplemented by contributions from independent researchers and scholars.

Today, the program includes regional and global studies of high performance, to take into account the explosive success of many emerging-market companies.

of new leadership blood and a continual shake-up of the top team.

Early Top-Team Renewal
Consider how the top team at Intel has evolved. Throughout its history, the semiconductor manufacturer has seen

its CEO mantle rest on five executives: Robert Noyce, Gordon Moore, Andy Grove, Craig Barrett, and current CEO Paul Otellini. Not once has the company had to look outside to find this talent, and the transitions have typically been orderly and well orchestrated. "We discuss executive changes 10 years out to identify gaps," explains David Yoffie, who has served on the Intel board since 1989.

Simple continuity is not Intel's goal in making changes at the top, however; evolving the business is. For instance, when Grove stepped down from the top spot, in 1998, he was still a highly effective leader. If continuity had been Intel's overwhelming concern, Grove might have stayed for another three years, until he reached the mandatory retirement age of 65. But instead, he handed the baton to Barrett, who then implemented a strategy for growing Intel's business through product extensions.

Indeed, each of Intel's CEOs has left his mark in a different way. Grove made the bold decision to move Intel away from memory chips in order to focus on microprocessors, a transition that established the company as a global high-tech leader. Since he took the helm, in 2005, Otellini has focused on the Atom mobile chip, which is being developed for use in just about any device that might need to connect to the web, including cell phones, navigation systems, and even sewing machines (for downloading patterns).

Through structured succession planning, Intel ensures that it chooses the CEO who is right for the challenges the company is facing, not simply the person next in line. And by changing CEOs early, the company gives its new leadership time to produce the reinvention needed, well before deteriorating revenues and dwindling options become a crisis.

Balance Short-Term and Long-Term Thinking

Ensuring that the team is balanced with a focus on both the present and the future is another critical step in developing a new capabilities curve. When Adobe bought Macromedia in 2005, then-CEO Bruce Chizen took a hard look at his senior managers to determine which of them had what it took to grow the company to annual revenues of $10 billion. What he found was a number of executives who lacked either the skills or the motivation to do what was necessary. Consequently, Chizen tapped more executives from Macromedia than from Adobe for key roles in the new organization. Those choices were based on Adobe's future needs, not on which executives were the most capable at the time.

Chizen wasn't tough-minded just with others. At the relatively young age of 52, and only seven years into his successful tenure, he handed over the reins to Shantanu Narayen, his longtime deputy. The timing might have seemed odd, but it made good sense for Adobe: The company faced a new set of challenges—and the need for new capabilities—as it anticipated going head-to-head against larger competitors like Microsoft.

In other cases, the executive team might need to gather fresh viewpoints from within the organization to balance long-established management thinking. Before Ratan Tata took over at India's Tata Group, in 1991, executives had comfortably ruled their fiefdoms for ages and rarely retired. But the new chairman began easing out those complacent executives (not surprisingly, some of their departures were acrimonious) and instituted a compulsory retirement age to help prevent the future stagnation of his senior leadership. The dramatic change opened dozens of opportunities for rising in-house talent who have helped Tata become India's largest private corporate group.

Organize to Avoid Overload

Finally, high performers organize their top teams so that responsibilities are more effectively divided and conquered. Three critical tasks of senior leadership are information sharing, consulting on important decisions, and making those decisions. Although many companies have one group that performs all three functions, this can easily become unwieldy.

An alternative approach, which we observed in many high performers, is to split those tasks—in effect, creating teams nested within teams. At the very top are the primary decision makers—a group of perhaps three to seven people. This group then receives advice from other teams, so hundreds of people may be providing important input.

Surplus Talent

Business reinvention requires not just nimble top teams but also large numbers of people ready to take on the considerable challenge of getting new businesses off the ground and making them thrive. High performers take an approach that is, in its way, as difficult as changing out top leadership before the company's main business has crested: They create much more talent than they need to run the current business effectively—particularly talent of the kind that can start and grow a business, not just manage one. This can be a hard sell in the best of times, which is probably why so many avoid it.

One of the signs that a company has surplus talent is that employees have time to think on the job. Many of our high performers make time to explore a regular component of their employees' workweek. (Think Google and 3M.) Another is a deep bench—one that allows promising managers to take on developmental assignments and not just get plugged in where there is an urgent need. High performance companies aggressively search out the right type of candidate and then take action to strengthen individuals for the challenges ahead.

Hire for Cultural Fit

High performance companies begin with the expectation that they are hiring people for the long term—a perspective that fundamentally alters the nature of their hiring and development practices. They don't just look for the best people for the current openings; they recognize that cultural fit is what helps ensure that someone will perform exceptionally well over time.

One company that gets this right is the Four Seasons Hotels and Resorts. It specifically looks for people who will thrive in a business that treats customers like kings—because, quite literally, some guests could be. "I can teach anyone to be a waiter," says Isadore Sharp, CEO of the luxury hotel chain in his book *Four Seasons: The Story of a Business Philosophy.* "But you can't change an ingrained poor attitude. We look for people who say, 'I'd be proud to be a doorman.'"

Reckitt Benckiser also puts cultural fit at the top of its hiring priorities. Before candidates begin the application process, they can complete an online simulation that determines whether they are likely to be a good match with the firm's exceptionally driven culture. The candidates are presented with business scenarios and asked how they would respond. After reviewing their "fit" score, they can decide for themselves whether they want to continue pursuing employment with the company.

Prepare for Challenges Ahead
Making sure that new employees are fit to successfully navigate the tough stretches in a long career requires something we call stressing for strength. At low-performer companies, employees may find themselves wilting when faced with unexpected or harsh terrain. High performers create environments—often challenging ones—in which employees acquire the skills and experience they will need to start the company's next S curve. The goal is partly to create what our Accenture colleague Bob Thomas, in his book on the topic, calls "crucible" experiences. These are life-changing events, whether on the job or not, whose lessons help transform someone into a leader.

Crucible experiences can—and should—be created intentionally. When Jeff Immelt was still in his early 30s and relatively new in his career at GE, he was tapped by then-CEO Jack Welch and HR chief Bill Conaty to deal with the problem of millions of faulty refrigerator compressors—despite his lack of familiarity with appliances or recalls. Immelt later said he would never have become CEO without that trial-by-fire experience.

Give Employees Room to Grow

After choosing and testing the right employees, companies must give them a chance to develop. To truly enable them to excel in their work, companies should take a hard look at exactly what people are required to do day by day.

UPS has long known that its truck drivers are crucial to its success. Experienced drivers know the fastest routes, taking into account the time of day, the weather, and various other factors. But the turnover rate for drivers was high, partly because of the hard physical labor required to load packages onto the trucks. So UPS separated out that task and gave it to part-time workers, who were more affordable and easier to find, allowing a valuable group of employees to concentrate on their capabilities and excel at their jobs.

Companies can also use organizational structure to provide employees with ample opportunities to grow. Illinois Tool Works, a global manufacturer of industrial products and equipment, is organized into more than 800 business units. Whenever one of those units becomes too large (the maximum size is around $50 million

Why Now?

Why Do Economic Slowdowns Call for Innovation and Reinvention?

Reduced sales and increased discounting tend to squash companies' revenue S curves. Worse, the S curves do not stretch back out as conditions improve. Companies lose ground in four key areas.

Intellectual Property

Patent offices don't put years back on the clock just because a company's sales tapered off in a bad economy. This can have a devastating effect on, for instance, pharmaceuticals, where generics constantly challenge proprietary drugs as patents expire.

Technology

Economic downturns can slow the introduction of new technologies, but not for long. Witness the fate of some manufacturers of plasma televisions, which have been forced to exit the business under the double whammy of the downturn and steady improvements in LCD and LED sets.

Competition

Companies looking to grow sales in a recession must take market share from competitors. As they press advantage, already weakened companies face possible extinction. In the movie-viewing market, for instance, companies that dominate newer channels have driven bricks-and-mortar retailers into bankruptcy.

Consumer Tastes

Novelty wears off, regardless of the economy. Even though they've bought less during the downturn, consumers accustomed to the idea of "fast fashion," for example, will not be interested in last year's styles.

in sales), ITW splits that business, thus opening up managerial positions for young talent. In fact, it's not uncommon for ITW managers to start running a business while they're still in their 20s.

And high performance businesses aren't afraid to leapfrog talented employees over those with longer tenure. After A.G. Lafley took over at P&G, for example, he needed someone to run the North American baby-care division, which was struggling. Instead of choosing one of the 78 general managers with seniority, he reached lower in the organization and tapped Deborah Henretta. Lafley's move paid off. Henretta reversed 20 years' worth of losses in the division and was later promoted to group president of Asia, overseeing a $4 billion-plus operation.

Breaking the mold in one way or another—as leaders have done at UPS, ITW, and P&G—is critical to building surplus talent in the organization. It not only keeps key individuals (or groups, in the case of UPS's drivers) on board; it also signals to the organization as a whole that no compromises on talent will be made in order to achieve short-sighted cost savings.

Even top organizations are vulnerable to slowdowns. In fact, an economic downturn can exacerbate problems for companies already nearing the end of their financial S curve. (See the sidebar "Why Now?") Even in the best of times, business crises—whether they are caused by hungry new competitors, transformational technology, or simply the aging of an industry or a company—come with regularity. Companies in other industries may be feeling great, while your business (or industry) faces its own great depression.

In the face of all these challenges, companies that manage themselves according to the three hidden S curves—the basis of competition, the distinctiveness of their capabilities, and a ready supply of talent—will be in a much better position to reinvent themselves, jumping to the next S curve with relative ease. Those that do not are likely to respond to a stall in growth by creating an urgent and drastic reinvention program—with little likelihood of success.

PAUL NUNES is the executive director of research at the Accenture Institute for High Performance. **TIM BREENE** is the CEO of Accenture Interactive, the company's digital marketing initiative. They are the authors of *Jumping the S-Curve: How to Beat the Growth Cycle, Get on Top, and Stay There* (Harvard Business Review Press, 2011), from which this article is adapted.

Originally published in January 2011. Reprint R1101D

Reinventing Your Business Model

by Mark W. Johnson, Clayton M. Christensen, and Henning Kagermann

IN 2003, APPLE INTRODUCED the iPod with the iTunes store, revolutionizing portable entertainment, creating a new market, and transforming the company. In just three years, the iPod/iTunes combination became a nearly $10 billion product, accounting for almost 50% of Apple's revenue. Apple's market capitalization catapulted from around $1 billion in early 2003 to over $150 billion by late 2007.

This success story is well known; what's less well known is that Apple was not the first to bring digital music players to market. A company called Diamond Multimedia introduced the Rio in 1998. Another firm, Best Data, introduced the Cabo 64 in 2000. Both products worked well and were portable and stylish. So why did the iPod, rather than the Rio or Cabo, succeed?

Apple did something far smarter than take a good technology and wrap it in a snazzy design. It took a good technology and wrapped it in a great business model. Apple's true innovation was to make download-ing digital music easy and convenient. To do that, the company built a groundbreaking business model that combined hardware, software, and service. This ap-proach worked like Gillette's famous blades-and-razor model in reverse: Apple essentially gave away the "blades" (low-margin iTunes music) to lock in purchase of the "razor" (the high-margin iPod). That model de-fined value in a new way and provided game-changing convenience to the consumer.

Business model innovations have reshaped entire in-dustries and redistributed billions of dollars of value. Retail discounters such as Wal-Mart and Target, which entered the market with pioneering business models, now account for 75% of the total valuation of the retail sector. Low-cost U.S. airlines grew from a blip on the radar screen to 55% of the market value of all carriers. Fully 11 of the 27 companies born in the last quarter cen-tury that grew their way into the *Fortune* 500 in the past 10 years did so through business model innovation.

Stories of business model innovation from well-established companies like Apple, however, are rare. An analysis of major innovations within existing corpo-rations in the past decade shows that precious few have been business-model related. And a recent Amer-ican Management Association study determined that no more than 10% of innovation investment at global companies is focused on developing new business models.

Yet everyone's talking about it. A 2005 survey by the Economist Intelligence Unit reported that over 50% of

Idea in Brief

When Apple introduced the iPod, it did something far smarter than wrap a good technology in a snazzy design. It wrapped a good technology in a **great business model**. Combining hardware, software, and service, the model provided game-changing convenience for consumers *and* record-breaking profits for Apple.

Great business models can reshape industries and drive spectacular growth. Yet many companies find business-model innovation difficult. Managers don't understand their existing model well enough to know when it needs changing—or how.

To determine whether your firm should alter its business model, Johnson, Christensen, and Kagermann advise these steps:

1. Articulate what makes your existing model successful. For example, what customer problem does it solve? How does it make money for your firm?

2. Watch for signals that your model needs changing, such as tough new competitors on the horizon.

3. Decide whether reinventing your model is worth the effort. The answer's yes only if the new model changes the industry or market.

executives believe business model innovation will become even more important for success than product or service innovation. A 2008 IBM survey of corporate CEOs echoed these results. Nearly all of the CEOs polled reported the need to adapt their business models; more than two-thirds said that extensive changes were required. And in these tough economic times, some CEOs are already looking to business model innovation to address permanent shifts in their market landscapes.

Senior managers at incumbent companies thus confront a frustrating question: Why is it so difficult to pull off the new growth that business model innovation can

Idea in Practice

Understand Your Current Business Model

A successful model has these components:

- **Customer value proposition.** The model helps customers perform a specific "job" that alternative offerings don't address.

  Example: MinuteClinics enable people to visit a doctor's office without appointments by making nurse practitioners available to treat minor health issues.

- **Profit formula.** The model generates value for your company through factors such as revenue model, cost structure, margins, and inventory turnover.

  Example: The Tata Group's inexpensive car, the Nano, is profitable because the company has reduced many cost structure elements, accepted lower-than-standard gross margins, and sold the Nano in large volumes to its target market: first-time car buyers in emerging markets.

- **Key resources and processes.** Your company has the people, technology, products, facilities, equipment, and brand required to deliver the value proposition to your targeted customers. And it has processes (training, manufacturing, service) to leverage those resources.

  Example: For Tata Motors to fulfill the requirements of the Nano's profit formula, it had to reconceive how a car is designed, manufactured, and distributed. It redefined its supplier strategy, choosing to outsource a remarkable 85% of the Nano's components and to use nearly 60% fewer vendors than normal to reduce transaction costs.

bring? Our research suggests two problems. The first is a lack of definition: Very little formal study has been done into the dynamics and processes of business model development. Second, few companies understand their existing business model well enough—the premise behind its development, its natural interdependencies, and its strengths and limitations. So they

Identify When a New Model May Be Needed

These circumstances often require business model change:

An *opportunity* to ...	Example
Address needs of large groups who find existing solutions too expensive or complicated.	The Nano's goal is to open car ownership to low-income consumers in emerging markets.
Capitalize on new technology, or leverage existing technologies in new markets.	A company develops a commercial application for a technology originally developed for military use.
Bring a job-to-be-done focus where it doesn't exist.	FedEx focused on performing customers' unmet "job": Receive packages faster and more reliably than any other service could.

A *need* to ...	Example
Fend off low-end disruptors.	Mini-mills threatened the integrated steel mills a generation ago by making steel at significantly lower prices.
Respond to shifts in competition.	Power-tool maker Hilti switched from selling to renting its tools in part because "good enough" low-end entrants had begun chipping away at the market for selling high-quality tools.

don't know when they can leverage their core business and when success requires a new business model.

After tackling these problems with dozens of companies, we have found that new business models often look unattractive to internal and external stakeholders—at the outset. To see past the borders of what is and into the land of the new, companies need a road map.

Ours consists of three simple steps. The first is to realize that success starts by not thinking about business models at all. It starts with thinking about the opportunity to satisfy a real customer who needs a job done. The second step is to construct a blueprint laying out how your company will fulfill that need at a profit. In our model, that plan has four elements. The third is to compare that model to your existing model to see how much you'd have to change it to capture the opportunity. Once you do, you will know if you can use your existing model and organization or need to separate out a new unit to execute a new model. Every successful company is already fulfilling a real customer need with an effective business model, whether that model is explicitly understood or not. Let's take a look at what that entails.

Business Model: A Definition

A business model, from our point of view, consists of four interlocking elements that, taken together, create and deliver value. The most important to get right, by far, is the first.

Customer Value Proposition (CVP)

A successful company is one that has found a way to create value for customers—that is, a way to help customers get an important job done. By "job" we mean a fundamental problem in a given situation that needs a solution. Once we understand the job and all its dimensions, including the full process for how to get it done, we can design the offering. The more important the job is to the customer, the lower the level of customer satisfaction with current options for getting the job done, and the better your solution is than existing alternatives at getting the job done (and, of course, the lower the price), the greater the CVP. Opportunities for creating a CVP are at their most potent, we have found, when alternative products and services have not been designed with the real job in mind and you can design an offering that gets that job—and only that job—done perfectly. We'll come back to that point later.

Profit formula

The profit formula is the blueprint that defines how the company creates value for itself while providing value to the customer. It consists of the following:

- **Revenue model:** price x volume

- **Cost structure:** direct costs, indirect costs, economies of scale. Cost structure will be predominantly driven by the cost of the key resources required by the business model.

- **Margin model:** given the expected volume and cost structure, the contribution needed from each transaction to achieve desired profits.

- **Resource velocity:** how fast we need to turn over inventory, fixed assets, and other assets—and, overall, how well we need to utilize resources— to support our expected volume and achieve our anticipated profits.

People often think the terms "profit formulas" and "business models" are interchangeable. But how you make a profit is only one piece of the model. We've found it most useful to start by setting the price required to deliver the CVP and then work backwards from there to determine what the variable costs and gross margins must be. This then determines what the scale and resource velocity needs to be to achieve the desired profits.

Key Resources

The key resources are assets such as the people, technology, products, facilities, equipment, channels, and brand required to deliver the value proposition to the targeted customer. The focus here is on the *key* elements that create value for the customer and the company, and the way those elements interact. (Every company also has generic resources that do not create competitive differentiation.)

Key Processes

Successful companies have operational and managerial processes that allow them to deliver value in a way they can successfully repeat and increase in scale. These may include such recurrent tasks as training, development, manufacturing, budgeting, planning, sales, and service. Key processes also include a company's rules, metrics, and norms.

These four elements form the building blocks of any business. The customer value proposition and the profit formula define value for the customer and the company, respectively; key resources and key processes describe how that value will be delivered to both the customer and the company.

As simple as this framework may seem, its power lies in the complex interdependencies of its parts. Major changes to any of these four elements affect the others and the whole. Successful businesses devise a more or less stable system in which these elements bond to one another in consistent and complementary ways.

How Great Models Are Built

To illustrate the elements of our business model framework, we will look at what's behind two companies' game-changing business model innovations.

Creating a Customer Value Proposition

It's not possible to invent or reinvent a business model without first identifying a clear customer value proposition. Often, it starts as a quite simple realization. Imagine, for a moment, that you are standing on a Mumbai road on a rainy day. You notice the large number of motor scooters snaking precariously in and out around the cars. As you look more closely, you see that most bear whole families—both parents and several children. Your first thought might be "That's crazy!" or "That's the way it is in developing countries—people get by as best they can."

When Ratan Tata of Tata Group looked out over this scene, he saw a critical job to be done: providing a safer alternative for scooter families. He understood that the cheapest car available in India cost easily five times what a scooter did and that many of these families could not afford one. Offering an affordable, safer, all-weather alternative for scooter families was a powerful value proposition, one with the potential to reach tens of millions of people who were not yet part of the car-buying market. Ratan Tata also recognized that Tata Motors' business model could not be used to develop such a product at the needed price point.

At the other end of the market spectrum, Hilti, a Liechtenstein-based manufacturer of high-end power tools for the construction industry, reconsidered the real job to be done for many of its current customers. A contractor makes money by finishing projects; if the required tools aren't available and functioning properly, the job doesn't get done. Contractors don't make money by *owning* tools; they make it by using them as efficiently as possible. Hilti could help contractors get the job done by selling tool *use* instead of the tools themselves—managing its customers' tool inventory by providing the best tool at the right time and quickly furnishing tool repairs, replacements, and upgrades, all for a monthly fee. To deliver on that value proposition, the company needed to create a fleet-management program for tools and in the process shift its focus from manufacturing and distribution to service. That meant Hilti had to construct a new profit formula and develop new resources and new processes.

The most important attribute of a customer value proposition is its precision: how perfectly it nails the customer job to be done—and nothing else. But such precision is often the most difficult thing to achieve. Companies trying to create the new often neglect to focus on *one* job; they dilute their efforts by attempting to do lots of things. In doing lots of things, they do nothing *really* well.

One way to generate a precise customer value proposition is to think about the four most common barriers keeping people from getting particular jobs done: insufficient wealth, access, skill, or time. Software maker Intuit devised QuickBooks to fulfill small-business owners' need to avoid running out of cash. By fulfilling that job with greatly simplified accounting software, Intuit broke the *skills barrier* that kept untrained small-business owners from using more-complicated accounting packages. MinuteClinic, the drugstore-based basic health care provider, broke the *time barrier* that kept people from visiting a doctor's office with minor health issues by making nurse practitioners available without appointments.

Designing a Profit Formula

Ratan Tata knew the only way to get families off their scooters and into cars would be to break the *wealth barrier* by drastically decreasing the price of the car. "What if I can change the game and make a car for one lakh?" Tata wondered, envisioning a price point of around US$2,500, less than half the price of the cheapest car available. This, of course, had dramatic ramifications for the profit formula: It required both a significant drop in gross margins and a radical reduction in many elements of the cost structure. He knew, however, he

The Elements of a Successful Business Model

EVERY SUCCESSFUL COMPANY already operates according to an effective business model. By systematically identifying all of its constituent parts, executives can understand how the model fulfills a potent value proposition in a profitable way using certain key resources and key processes. With that understanding, they can then judge how well the same model could be used to fulfill a radically different CVP—and what they'd need to do to construct a new one, if need be, to capitalize on that opportunity.

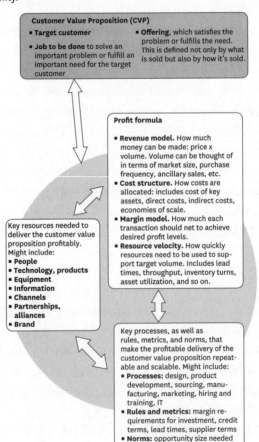

Customer Value Proposition (CVP)

- **Target customer**
- **Job to be done** to solve an important problem or fulfill an important need for the target customer
- **Offering**, which satisfies the problem or fulfills the need. This is defined not only by what is sold but also by how it's sold.

Profit formula

- **Revenue model.** How much money can be made: price x volume. Volume can be thought of in terms of market size, purchase frequency, ancillary sales, etc.
- **Cost structure.** How costs are allocated: includes cost of key assets, direct costs, indirect costs, economies of scale.
- **Margin model.** How much each transaction should net to achieve desired profit levels.
- **Resource velocity.** How quickly resources need to be used to support target volume. Includes lead times, throughput, inventory turns, asset utilization, and so on.

Key resources needed to deliver the customer value proposition profitably. Might include:
- **People**
- **Technology, products**
- **Equipment**
- **Information**
- **Channels**
- **Partnerships, alliances**
- **Brand**

Key processes, as well as rules, metrics, and norms, that make the profitable delivery of the customer value proposition repeatable and scalable. Might include:
- **Processes:** design, product development, sourcing, manufacturing, marketing, hiring and training, IT
- **Rules and metrics:** margin requirements for investment, credit terms, lead times, supplier terms
- **Norms:** opportunity size needed for investment, approach to customers and channels

could still make money if he could increase sales volume dramatically, and he knew that his target base of consumers was potentially huge.

For Hilti, moving to a contract management program required shifting assets from customers' balance sheets to its own and generating revenue through a lease/subscription model. For a monthly fee, customers could have a full complement of tools at their fingertips, with repair and maintenance included. This would require a fundamental shift in all major components of the profit formula: the revenue stream (pricing, the staging of payments, and how to think about volume), the cost structure (including added sales development and contract management costs), and the supporting margins and transaction velocity.

Identifying Key Resources and Processes

Having articulated the value proposition for both the customer and the business, companies must then consider the key resources and processes needed to deliver that value. For a professional services firm, for example, the key resources are generally its people, and the key processes are naturally people related (training and development, for instance). For a packaged goods company, strong brands and well-selected channel retailers might be the key resources, and associated brand-building and channel-management processes among the critical processes.

Oftentimes, it's not the individual resources and processes that make the difference but their relationship to one another. Companies will almost always

Hilti Sidesteps Commoditization

HILTI IS CAPITALIZING on a game-changing opportunity to increase profitability by turning products into a service. Rather than sell tools (at lower and lower prices), it's selling a "just-the-tool-you-need-when-you-need-it, no-repair-or-storage-hassles" service. Such a radical change in customer value proposition required a shift in all parts of its business model.

Traditional power tool company		Hilti's tool fleet management service
Sales of industrial and professional power tools and accessories	Customer value proposition	Leasing a comprehensive fleet of tools to increase contractors' on-site productivity
Low margins, high inventory turnover	Profit formula	Higher margins; asset heavy; monthly payments for tool maintenance, repair, and replacement
Distribution channel, low-cost manufacturing plants in developing countries, R&D	Key resources and processes	Strong direct-sales approach, contract management, IT systems for inventory management and repair, warehousing

need to integrate their key resources and processes in a unique way to get a job done perfectly for a set of customers. When they do, they almost always create enduring competitive advantage. Focusing first on the value proposition and the profit formula makes clear how those resources and processes need to interrelate. For example, most general hospitals offer a value proposition that might be described as, "We'll do anything for anybody." Being all things to all people requires these hospitals to have a vast collection of resources (specialists, equipment, and so on) that can't be knit together in any proprietary way. The result is not just a lack of differentiation but dissatisfaction.

By contrast, a hospital that focuses on a specific value proposition can integrate its resources and processes in a unique way that delights customers. National Jewish Health in Denver, for example, is organized around a focused value proposition we'd characterize as, "If you have a disease of the pulmonary system, bring it here. We'll define its root cause and prescribe an effective therapy." Narrowing its focus has allowed National Jewish to develop processes that integrate the ways in which its specialists and specialized equipment work together.

For Tata Motors to fulfill the requirements of its customer value proposition and profit formula for the Nano, it had to reconceive how a car is designed, manufactured, and distributed. Tata built a small team of fairly young engineers who would not, like the company's more-experienced designers, be influenced and constrained in their thinking by the automaker's existing profit formulas. This team dramatically minimized the number of parts in the vehicle, resulting in a significant cost saving. Tata also reconceived its supplier strategy, choosing to outsource a remarkable 85% of the Nano's components and use nearly 60% fewer vendors than normal to reduce transaction costs and achieve better economies of scale.

At the other end of the manufacturing line, Tata is envisioning an entirely new way of assembling and distributing its cars. The ultimate plan is to ship the modular components of the vehicles to a combined network of company-owned and independent entrepreneur-owned assembly plants, which will build them to order. The Nano will be designed, built, distributed, and serviced in a radically new way—one that could not be accomplished without a new business model. And while the jury is still out, Ratan Tata may solve a traffic safety problem in the process.

For Hilti, the greatest challenge lay in training its sales representatives to do a thoroughly new task. Fleet management is not a half-hour sale; it takes days, weeks, even months of meetings to persuade customers to buy a program instead of a product. Suddenly, field reps accustomed to dealing with crew leaders and on-site purchasing managers in mobile trailers found themselves staring down CEOs and CFOs across conference tables.

Additionally, leasing required new resources— new people, more robust IT systems, and other new technologies—to design and develop the appropriate packages and then come to an agreement on monthly payments. Hilti needed a process for maintaining large arsenals of tools more inexpensively and effectively than its customers had. This required warehousing, an inventory management system, and a supply of replacement tools. On the customer management side, Hilti developed a website that enabled construction managers to view all the tools in their fleet and their usage rates. With that information readily available, the managers could easily handle the cost accounting associated with those assets.

Rules, norms, and metrics are often the last element to emerge in a developing business model. They may not be fully envisioned until the new product or service has been road tested. Nor should they be. Business models need to have the flexibility to change in their early years.

When a New Business Model Is Needed

Established companies should not undertake business-model innovation lightly. They can often create new products that disrupt competitors without fundamentally changing their own business model. Procter & Gamble, for example, developed a number of what it calls "disruptive market innovations" with such products as the Swiffer disposable mop and duster and Febreze, a new kind of air freshener. Both innovations built on P&G's existing business model and its established dominance in household consumables.

There are clearly times, however, when creating new growth requires venturing not only into unknown market territory but also into unknown business model territory. When? The short answer is "When significant changes are needed to all four elements of your existing model." But it's not always that simple. Management judgment is clearly required. That said, we have observed five strategic circumstances that often require business model change:

1. The opportunity to address through disruptive innovation the needs of large groups of potential customers who are shut out of a market entirely because existing solutions are too expensive or complicated for them. This includes the opportunity to democratize products in emerging markets (or reach the bottom of the pyramid), as Tata's Nano does.

2. The opportunity to capitalize on a brand-new technology by wrapping a new business model around

it (Apple and MP3 players) or the opportunity to leverage a tested technology by bringing it to a whole new market (say, by offering military technologies in the commercial space or vice versa).

3. The opportunity to bring a job-to-be-done focus where one does not yet exist. That's common in industries where companies focus on products or customer segments, which leads them to refine existing products more and more, increasing commoditization over time. A jobs focus allows companies to redefine industry profitability. For example, when FedEx entered the package delivery market, it did not try to compete through lower prices or better marketing. Instead, it concentrated on fulfilling an entirely unmet customer need to receive packages far, far faster, and more reliably, than any service then could. To do so, it had to integrate its key processes and resources in a vastly more efficient way. The business model that resulted from this job-to-be-done emphasis gave FedEx a significant competitive advantage that took UPS many years to copy.

4. The need to fend off low-end disrupters. If the Nano is successful, it will threaten other automobile makers, much as mini-mills threatened the integrated steel mills a generation ago by making steel at significantly lower cost.

5. The need to respond to a shifting basis of competition. Inevitably, what defines an acceptable

solution in a market will change over time, leading core market segments to commoditize. Hilti needed to change its business model in part because of lower global manufacturing costs; "good enough" low-end entrants had begun chipping away at the market for high-quality power tools.

Of course, companies should not pursue business model reinvention unless they are confident that the opportunity is large enough to warrant the effort. And, there's really no point in instituting a new business model unless it's not only new to the company but in some way new or game-changing to the industry or market. To do otherwise would be a waste of time and money.

These questions will help you evaluate whether the challenge of business model innovation will yield acceptable results. Answering "yes" to all four greatly increases the odds of successful execution:

- Can you nail the job with a focused, compelling customer value proposition?

- Can you devise a model in which all the elements—the customer value proposition, the profit formula, the key resources, and the key processes—work together to get the job done in the most efficient way possible?

- Can you create a new business development process unfettered by the often negative influences of your core business?

- Will the new business model disrupt competitors?

Dow Corning Embraces the Low End

TRADITIONALLY HIGH-MARGIN DOW CORNING found new opportunities in low-margin offerings by setting up a separate business unit that operates in an entirely different way. By fundamentally differentiating its low-end and high-end offerings, the company avoided cannibalizing its traditional business even as it found new profits at the low end.

Established business		New business unit
Customized solutions, negotiated contracts	Customer value proposition	No frills, bulk prices, sold through the internet
High-margin, high-overhead retail prices pay for value-added services	Profit formula	Spot-market pricing, low overhead to accommodate lower margins, high throughput
R&D, sales, and service orientation	Key resources and processes	IT system, lowest-cost processes, maximum automation

Creating a new model for a new business does not mean the current model is threatened or should be changed. A new model often reinforces and complements the core business, as Dow Corning discovered.

How Dow Corning Got Out of Its Own Way

When business model innovation is clearly called for, success lies not only in getting the model right but also in making sure the incumbent business doesn't in some way prevent the new model from creating value or thriving. That was a problem for Dow Corning when it built a new business unit—with a new profit formula—from scratch.

For many years, Dow Corning had sold thousands of silicone-based products and provided sophisticated technical services to an array of industries. After years of profitable growth, however, a number of product areas were stagnating. A strategic review uncovered a critical insight: Its low-end product segment was commoditizing. Many customers experienced in silicone application no longer needed technical services; they needed basic products at low prices. This shift created an opportunity for growth, but to exploit that opportunity Dow Corning had to figure out a way to serve these customers with a lower-priced product. The problem was that both the business model and the culture were built on high-priced, innovative product and service packages. In 2002, in pursuit of what was essentially a commodity business for low-end customers, Dow Corning CEO Gary Anderson asked executive Don Sheets to form a team to start a new business.

The team began by formulating a customer value proposition that it believed would fulfill the job to be done for these price-driven customers. It determined that the price point had to drop 15% (which for a commoditizing material was a huge reduction). As the team analyzed what that new customer value proposition would require, it realized reaching that point was going to take a lot more than merely eliminating services. Dramatic price reduction would call for a different profit formula with a fundamentally lower cost structure, which depended heavily on developing a new IT system. To sell more products faster, the company would need to use the internet to automate processes and reduce overhead as much as possible.

When the Old Model Will Work

YOU DON'T ALWAYS NEED A new business model to capitalize on a game-changing opportunity. Sometimes, as P&G did with its Swiffer, a company finds that its current model is revolutionary in a new market. When will the old model do? When you can fulfill the new customer value proposition:

- With your current profit formula
- Using most, if not all, of your current key resources and processes
- Using the same core metrics, rules, and norms you now use to run your business

Breaking the Rules

As a mature and successful company, Dow Corning was full of highly trained employees used to delivering its high-touch, customized value proposition. To automate, the new business would have to be far more standardized, which meant instituting different and, overall, much stricter rules. For example, order sizes would be limited to a few, larger-volume options; order lead times would fall between two and four weeks (exceptions would cost extra); and credit terms would be fixed. There would be charges if a purchaser required customer service. The writing was on the wall: The new venture would be low-touch, self-service, and standardized. To succeed, Dow Corning would have to break the rules that had previously guided its success.

Sheets next had to determine whether this new venture, with its new rules, could succeed within the confines of Dow Corning's core enterprise. He set up an experimental war game to test how existing staff and systems would react to the requirements of the new customer value proposition. He got crushed as entrenched habits and existing processes thwarted any attempt to change the game. It became clear that the corporate antibodies would kill the initiative before it got off the ground. The way forward was clear: The new venture had to be free from existing rules and free to decide what rules would be appropriate in order for the new commodity line of business to thrive. To nurture the opportunity—and also protect the existing model—a new business unit with a new brand identity was needed. Xiameter was born.

Identifying New Competencies
Following the articulation of the new customer value proposition and new profit formula, the Xiameter team focused on the new competencies it would need, its key resources and processes. Information technology, just a small part of Dow Corning's core competencies at that time, emerged as an essential part of the now web-enabled business. Xiameter also needed employees who could make smart decisions very quickly and who would thrive in a fast-changing environment, filled initially with lots of ambiguity. Clearly, new abilities would have to be brought into the business.

Although Xiameter would be established and run as a separate business unit, Don Sheets and the Xiameter team did not want to give up the incumbency advantage that deep knowledge of the industry and of their own products gave them. The challenge was to tap into the expertise without importing the old-rules mind-set.

What Rules, Norms, and Metrics Are Standing in Your Way?

IN ANY BUSINESS, a fundamental understanding of the core model often fades into the mists of institutional memory, but it lives on in rules, norms, and metrics put in place to protect the status quo (for example, "Gross margins must be at 40%"). They are the first line of defense against any new model's taking root in an existing enterprise.

Financial

- Gross margins
- Opportunity size
- Unit pricing
- Unit margin
- Time to breakeven
- Net present value calculations
- Fixed cost investment
- Credit items

Sheets conducted a focused HR search within Dow Corning for risk takers. During the interview process, when he came across candidates with the right skills, he asked them to take the job on the spot, before they left the room. This approach allowed him to cherry-pick those who could make snap decisions and take big risks.

The Secret Sauce: Patience
Successful new businesses typically revise their business models four times or so on the road to profitability.

Operational

- End-product quality
- Supplier quality
- Owned versus outsourced manufacturing
- Customer service
- Channels
- Lead times
- Throughput

Other

- Pricing
- Performance demands
- Product-development life cycles
- Basis for individuals' rewards and incentives
- Brand parameters

While a well-considered business-model-innovation process can often shorten this cycle, successful incumbents must tolerate initial failure and grasp the need for course correction. In effect, companies have to focus on learning and adjusting as much as on executing. We recommend companies with new business models be patient for growth (to allow the market opportunity to unfold) but impatient for profit (as an early validation that the model works). A profitable business is the best early indication of a viable model.

Accordingly, to allow for the trial and error that naturally accompanies the creation of the new while also constructing a development cycle that would produce results and demonstrate feasibility with minimal resource outlay, Dow Corning kept the scale of Xiameter's operation small but developed an aggressive timetable for launch and set the goal of becoming profitable by the end of year one.

Xiameter paid back Dow Corning's investment in just three months and went on to become a major, transformative success. Beforehand, Dow Corning had had no online sales component; now 30% of sales originate online, nearly three times the industry average. Most of these customers are new to the company. Far from cannibalizing existing customers, Xiameter has actually supported the main business, allowing Dow Corning's salespeople to more easily enforce premium pricing for their core offerings while providing a viable alternative for the price-conscious.

———————

Established companies' attempts at transformative growth typically spring from product or technology innovations. Their efforts are often characterized by prolonged development cycles and fitful attempts to find a market. As the Apple iPod story that opened this article suggests, truly transformative businesses are never exclusively about the discovery and commercialization of a great technology. Their success comes from enveloping the new technology in an appropriate, powerful business model.

Bob Higgins, the founder and general partner of Highland Capital Partners, has seen his share of venture success and failure in his 20 years in the industry. He sums up the importance and power of business model innovation this way: "I think historically where we [venture capitalists] fail is when we back technology. Where we succeed is when we back new business models."

MARK W. JOHNSON is the author of *Seizing the White Space* (Harvard Business Review Press, 2009). He is also the chairman of Innosight, an innovation strategy firm he cofounded with **CLAYTON M. CHRISTENSEN,** the Robert and Jane Cizik Professor of Business Administration at Harvard Business School. **HENNING KAGERMANN** is the co-CEO of SAP AG in Germany.

Originally published in December 2008. Reprint R0812C

Why Business Models Matter

by Joan Magretta

"BUSINESS MODEL" WAS ONE of the great buzzwords of the Internet boom, routinely invoked, as the writer Michael Lewis put it, "to glorify all manner of half-baked plans." A company didn't need a strategy, or a special competence, or even any customers—all it needed was a Web-based business model that promised wild profits in some distant, ill-defined future. Many people—investors, entrepreneurs, and executives alike—bought the fantasy and got burned. And as the inevitable counterreaction played out, the concept of the business model fell out of fashion nearly as quickly as the .com appendage itself.

That's a shame. For while it's true that a lot of capital was raised to fund flawed business models, the fault lies not with the concept of the business model but with its distortion and misuse. A good business model remains essential to every successful organization, whether it's a new venture or an established player. But before managers can apply the concept, they need a simple working definition that clears up the fuzziness associated with the term.

Telling a Good Story

The word "model" conjures up images of white boards covered with arcane mathematical formulas. Business models, though, are anything but arcane. They are, at heart, stories—stories that explain how enterprises work. A good business model answers Peter Drucker's age-old questions: Who is the customer? And what does the customer value? It also answers the fundamental questions every manager must ask: How do we make money in this business? What is the underlying economic logic that explains how we can deliver value to customers at an appropriate cost?

Consider the story behind one of the most successful business models of all time: that of the traveler's check. During a European vacation in 1892, J.C. Fargo, the president of American Express, had a hard time translating his letters of credit into cash. "The moment I got off the beaten path," he said on his return, "they were no more use than so much wet wrapping paper. If the president of American Express has that sort of trouble, just think what ordinary travelers face. Something has got to be done about it."[1] What American Express did was to create the traveler's check—and from that innovation evolved a robust business model with all the elements of a good story: precisely delineated characters, plausible motivations, and a plot that turns on an insight about value.

Idea in Brief

The terms "business model" and "strategy" are among the most sloppily used in business. People use them interchangeably to refer to *everything*—so they mean nothing.

But no organization can afford fuzzy thinking about these fundamental concepts. A business model and a strategy are two different animals. One explains who your customers are and how you plan to make money by providing them with value; the other, how you'll beat competitors by being different.

A well-thought-out business model also enables you to test and revise your assumptions about customers, think rigorously about your business, and align employees behind your company's mission.

Sure, the business-model concept unraveled after flagrant misuse by dot bombs. But when you build a *sound* model that complements your strategy, you equip your company to beat even your toughest rivals.

The story was straightforward for customers. In exchange for a small fee, travelers could buy both peace of mind (the checks were insured against loss and theft) and convenience (they were very widely accepted). Merchants also played a key role in the tale. They accepted the checks because they trusted the American Express name, which was like a universal letter of credit, and because, by accepting them, they attracted more customers. The more other merchants accepted the checks, the stronger any individual merchant's motivation became not to be left out.

As for American Express, it had discovered a riskless business, because customers always paid cash for the checks. Therein lies the twist to the plot, the underlying economic logic that turned what would have been an unremarkable operation into a money machine.

Idea in Practice

Two Tests

Powerful business models pass two tests:

1. **The narrative test:** The business model tells a logical story explaining who your customers are, what they value, and how you'll make money providing them that value.

   The story's plot may turn on one of two links in the generic business value chain:

   - **making something that satisfies an unmet need;** e.g., American Express traveler's checks gave travelers new peace of mind

   - **selling something in innovative ways;** e.g., Eastern Exclusives distributes restaurant discount-coupon books in bulk to university housing

   departments, which distribute them free to dorms

2. **The numbers test:** A business model's story holds up only if you tie assumptions about customers to sound economics—your P&L must add up. For example, on-line grocery models failed because customers declined to pay substantially more on-line than in stores. E-grocers couldn't cover their marketing, technology, and delivery costs.

   Failing *either* test can prove fatal.

   Example: When EuroDisney opened its Paris theme park, it assumed Europeans were like Americans. But instead of grazing all day at the park's restaurants, Europeans wanted to eat meals at the

The twist was *float*. In most businesses, costs precede revenues: Before anyone can buy your product, you've got to build it and pay for it. The traveler's check turned the cycle of debt and risk on its head. Because people paid the checks before (often long before) they used them, American Express was getting something banks had long enjoyed—the equivalent of an interest-free loan from its customers. Moreover, some of the checks were never cashed, giving the company an extra windfall.

same hour. Results? Overloaded restaurants, long lines, frustrated patrons. EuroDisney's model failed the narrative test because it misunderstood customers' motivations.

Models *passing* both tests clarify how your business's various elements fit together.

Example: On-line auction giant eBay combined a compelling narrative with major profit potential. This on-line business "couldn't be done offline" and still provide value to collectors, bargain hunters, and small-business people. Its narrow scope of activities creates a highly profitable cost structure. For example, sellers and buyers handle payment and shipping logistics—so eBay incurs no inventory or transportation costs and avoids credit risk.

A Strategy Complement

Having a solid business model isn't enough. You also need a strategy, to plan how you'll beat your rivals—by being different.

Example: Wal-Mart used Kmart's **business model**—but implemented a unique **strategy**: Rather than trying to be just like its rivals, it promised *different* value to customers in *different* markets. It put big discount stores into "little one-horse towns" that competitors ignored. Founder Sam Walton bet—rightly—that if his stores beat city prices by offering name brands (not second-tier, private-label brands), townspeople would "shop [close to] home."

As this story shows, a successful business model represents a better way than the existing alternatives. It may offer more value to a discrete group of customers. Or it may completely replace the old way of doing things and become the standard for the next generation of entrepreneurs to beat. Nobody today would head off on vacation armed with a suitcase full of letters of credit. Fargo's business model changed the rules of the game, in this case, the economics of travel. By eliminating the fear of being robbed and the hours spent trying to get cash in a strange city, the checks removed a significant barrier to travel, helping many more people to take many more trips. Like all really powerful business models, this one didn't just shift existing revenues among companies; it created new, incremental demand. Traveler's checks remained the preferred method for taking money abroad for decades, until a new technology—the automated teller machine—granted travelers even greater convenience.

Creating a business model is, then, a lot like writing a new story. At some level, all new stories are variations on old ones, reworkings of the universal themes underlying all human experience. Similarly, all new business models are variations on the generic value chain underlying all businesses. Broadly speaking, this chain has two parts. Part one includes all the activities associated with making something: designing it, purchasing raw materials, manufacturing, and so on. Part two includes all the activities associated with selling something: finding and reaching customers, transacting a sale, distributing the product or delivering the service. A new business model's plot may turn on designing a new product for an unmet need, as it did with the traveler's check. Or it may turn a process innovation, a better way of making or selling or distributing an already proven product or service.

Think about the simple business that direct-marketing pioneer Michael Bronner created in 1980 when he was a junior at Boston University. Like his classmates, Bronner had occasionally bought books of discount coupons for local stores and restaurants. Students paid a small fee for the coupon books. But Bronner had a better idea. Yes, the books created value for students, but they had the potential to create much more value for merchants, who stood to gain by increasing their sales of pizza and haircuts. Bronner realized that the key to unlocking that potential was wider distribution—putting a coupon book in every student's backpack.

That posed two problems. First, as Bronner well knew students were often strapped for cash. Giving the books away for free would solve that problem. Second, Bronner needed to get the books to students at a cost that wouldn't eat up his profits. So he made a clever proposal to the dean of Boston University's housing department: Bronner would assemble the coupon books and deliver them in bulk to the housing department, and the department could distribute them free to every dorm on campus. This would make the department look good in the eyes of the students, a notoriously tough crowd to please. The dean agreed.

Now Bronner could make an even more interesting proposal to neighborhood business owners. If they agreed to pay a small fee to appear in the new book, their coupons would be seen by all 14,000 residents of BU's dorms. Bronner's idea took off. Before long, he had extended the concept to other campuses, then to downtown office buildings. Eastern Exclusives, his first company, was born. His innovation wasn't the coupon book but his business model; it worked because he had insight into the motivations of three sets of characters: students, merchants, and school administrators.

Tying Narrative to Numbers

The term "business model" first came into widespread use with the advent of the personal computer and the spreadsheet. Before the spreadsheet, business planning usually meant producing a single, base-case forecast. At best, you did a little sensitivity analysis around the projection. The spreadsheet ushered in a much more analytic approach to planning because every major line item could be pulled apart, its components and subcomponents analyzed and tested. You could ask what-if questions about the critical assumptions on which your business depended—for example, what if customers are more price-sensitive than we thought?—and with a few keystrokes, you could see how any change would play out on every aspect of the whole. In other words, you could model the behavior of a business.

This was something new. Before the personal computer changed the nature of business planning, most successful business models, like Fargo's, were created more by accident than by design and forethought. The business model became clear only after the fact. By enabling companies to tie their marketplace insights much more tightly to the resulting economics—to link their assumptions about how people would behave to the numbers of a pro forma P&L—spreadsheets made it possible to model businesses *before* they were launched.

Of course, a spreadsheet is only as good as the assumptions that go into it. Once an enterprise starts operating, the underlying assumptions of its model—about both the motivations and economics—are subjected to continuous testing in the marketplace. And success often hinges on management's ability to tweak, or even overhaul, the model on the fly. When EuroDisney opened its Paris theme park in 1992, it borrowed the business model that had worked so well in Disney's U.S. parks. Europeans, the company thought, would spend roughly the same amount of time and money per visit as Americans did on food, rides, and souvenirs.

Each of Disney's assumptions about the revenue side of the business turned out to be wrong. Europeans did not, for example, graze all day long at the park's various restaurants the way Americans did. Instead, they all expected to seated at precisely the same lunch or dinner hour, which overloaded the facilities and created long lines of frustrated patrons. Because of those miscalculations, EuroDisney was something of a disaster in its early years. It became a success only after a dozen or so of the key elements in its business model were changed, one by one.

When managers operate consciously from a model of how the entire business system will work, every decision, initiative, and measurement provides valuable feedback. Profits are important not only for their own sake but also because they tell you whether your model is working. If you fail to achieve the results you expected, you reexamine your model, as EuroDisney did. Business modeling is, in this sense, the managerial equivalent of the scientific method—you start with a hypothesis, which you then test in action and revise when necessary.

Two Critical Tests

When business models don't work, it's because they fail either the narrative test (the story doesn't make sense) or the numbers test (the P&L doesn't add up). The business model of on-line grocers, for instance, failed the numbers test. The grocery industry has very thin margins to begin with, and on-line merchants like Webvan incurred new costs for marketing, service, delivery, and technology. Since customers weren't willing to pay significantly more for groceries bought on-line than in stores, there was no way the math could work. Internet grocers had plenty of company. Many ventures in the first wave of electronic commerce failed simply because the basic business math was flawed.

Other business models failed the narrative test. Consider the rapid rise and fall of Priceline Webhouse Club. This was an offshoot of Priceline.com, the company that introduced name-your-own pricing to the purchase of airline tickets. Wall Street's early enthusiasm encouraged CEO Jay Walker to extend his concept to groceries and gasoline.

Here's the story Walker tried to tell. Via the Web, millions of consumers would tell him how much they wanted to pay for, say, a jar of peanut butter. Consumers could specify the price but not the brand, so they might end up with Jif or they might end up with Skippy. Webhouse would then aggregate the bids and go to companies like P&G and Bestfoods and try to make a deal: Take 50 cents off the price of your peanut butter, and we'll order a million jars this week. Webhouse wanted to be a power broker for individual consumers: Representing millions of shoppers, it would negotiate discounts and then pass on the savings to its customers, taking a fee in the process.

What was wrong with the story? It assumed that companies like P&G, Kimberly-Clark, and Exxon wanted to play this game. Think about that for a minute. Big consumer companies have spent decades and billions of dollars building brand loyalty. The Webhouse model teaches consumers to buy on price alone. So why would the manufacturers want to help Webhouse undermine both their prices and the brand identities they'd worked so hard to build? They wouldn't. The story just didn't make sense. To be a power broker, Webhouse needed a huge base of loyal customers. To get those customers, it first needed to deliver discounts. Since the consumer product companies refused to play, Webhouse had to pay for those discounts out of its own pocket. A few hundred million dollars later, in October 2000, it ran out of cash—and out of investors who still believed the story.

In case anyone thinks that Internet entrepreneurs have a monopoly on flawed business models, think again. We tend to forget about ideas that don't pan out, but business history is littered with them. In the 1980s, the one-stop financial supermarket was a business model that fired the imagination of many executives— but Sears, to cite one example, discovered that its customers just didn't get the connection between power tools and annuities. In the 1990s, Silicon Graphics invested hundreds of millions of dollars in interactive television, but it was unable to find real customers who were as enchanted by the technology as the engineers who invented it. Ultimately, models like these fail because they are built on faulty assumptions about customer behavior. They are solutions in search of a problem.

The irony about the slipshod use of the concept of business models is that when used correctly, it actually forces managers to think rigorously about their businesses. A business model's great strength as a planning tool is that it focuses attention on how all the elements of the system fit into a working whole. It's no surprise that, even during the Internet boom, executives who grasped the basics of business model thinking were in a better position to lead the winners. Meg Whitman, for example, joined eBay in its early days because she was struck by what she described as "the emotional connection between eBay users and the site."[1] The way people behaved was an early indicator of the potential power of the eBay brand. Whitman also realized that eBay, unlike many Internet businesses that were being created, simply "couldn't be done off-line." In other words, Whitman—a seasoned executive—saw a compelling, coherent narrative with the potential to be translated into a profitable business.

Whitman has remained attentive to the psychology and the economics that draw collectors, bargain hunters, community seekers, and small-business people to eBay. Its auction model succeeds not just because the Internet lowers the cost of connecting vast numbers of buyers and sellers but also because eBay has made decisions about the scope of its activities that result in an appropriate cost structure. After an auction, eBay leaves it to the sellers and buyers to work out the logistics of payment and shipping. The company never takes possession of the goods or carries any inventory. It incurs no transportation costs. It bears no credit risk. And it has none of the overhead that would come with those activities.

What About Strategy?

Every viable organization is built on a sound business model, whether or not its founders or its managers conceive of what they do in those terms. But a business model isn't the same thing as a strategy, even though many people use the terms interchangeably today. Business models describe, as a system, how the pieces of a business fit together. But they don't factor in one critical dimension of performance: competition. Sooner or later—and it is usually sooner—every enterprise runs into competitors. Dealing with that reality is strategy's job.

A competitive strategy explains how you will do better than your rivals. And doing better, by definition, means being different. Organizations achieve superior performance when they are unique, when they do something no other business does in ways that no other business can duplicate. When you cut away the jargon, that's what strategy is all about—how you are going to do better by being different. The logic is straightforward: When all companies offer the same products and services to the same customers by performing the same kinds of activities, no company will prosper. Customers will benefit, at least in the short term, while head-to-head competition drives prices down to a point where returns are inadequate. It was precisely this kind of competition—destructive competition, to use Michael Porter's term—that did in many Internet retailers, whether they were selling pet supplies, drugs, or toys. Too many fledgling companies rushed to market with identical business models and no strategies to differentiate themselves in terms of which customers and markets to serve, what products and services to offer, and what kinds of value to create.

To see the distinction between a strategy and a business model, you need only look at Wal-Mart. You might think that the giant retailer's success was a result of pioneering a new business model, but that's not the case. When Sam Walton opened his first Wal-Mart in 1962 in the hamlet of Rogers, Arkansas, the discount-retailing business model had been around for a few years. It had emerged in the mid-1950s, when a slew of industry pioneers (now long forgotten) began to apply supermarket logic to the sale of general merchandise. Supermarkets had been educating customers since the 1930s about the value of giving up personal service in exchange for lower food prices, and the new breed of retailers saw that they could adapt the basic story line of the supermarket to clothing, appliances, and a host of other consumer goods. The idea was to offer lower prices than conventional department stores by slashing costs. And so the basic business model for discount retailing took shape: First, strip away the department store's physical amenities such as the carpeting and the chandeliers. Second, configure the stores to handle large numbers of shoppers efficiently. And third, put fewer salespeople on the floor and rely on customers to serve themselves. Do those things well, and you could offer low prices and still make money.

Walton heard about the new discount stores, visited a few, and liked their potential. In 1962, he decided to set out on his own, borrowing a lot of ideas for his early stores from Kmart and others. But it was what he chose to do differently—the ways he put his own stamp on the basic business model—that made Wal-Mart so fabulously successful. His model was the same as Kmart's, but his strategy was unique.

From the very start, for instance, Walton chose to serve a different group of customers in a different set of markets. The ten largest discounters in 1962, all gone today, focused on large metropolitan areas and cities like New York. Wal-Mart's "key strategy," in Walton's own words, "was to put good-sized stores into little one-horse towns which everybody else was ignoring."[1] He sought out isolated rural towns, like Rogers, with populations between 5,000 and 25,000. Being a small-town guy himself, Walton knew the terrain well. The nearest city was probably a four-hour drive away. He rightly bet that if his stores could match or beat the city prices, "people would shop at home." And since Wal-Mart's markets tended to be too small to support more than one large retailer, Walton was able to preempt competitors and discourage them from entering Wal-Mart's territory.

Wal-Mart also took a different approach to merchandising and pricing than its competitors did—that is, it promised customers a different kind of value. While competitors relied heavily on private label goods, second-tier brands, and price promotions, Wal-Mart promised national brands at everyday low prices. To make this promise more than a marketing slogan, the company pursued efficiency and reduced costs through innovative practices in areas such as purchasing, logistics, and information management.

The business model of discount retailing has attracted many players since it emerged in the 1950s. Most of them have failed. A few, like Wal-Mart and Target, have achieved superior performance over the long haul because their strategies set them apart. Wal-Mart offers branded goods for less to a carefully chosen customer base. Target built a strategy around a different kind of value—style and fashion. The losers in the industry—the chronic underperformers like Kmart—are companies that tried to be all things to all people. They failed to find distinctive ways to compete.

A Good Model Is Not Enough

There's another, more recent story that sheds further light on the relationship between business models and strategies. It's the story of Dell Computer. Unlike Sam Walton, Michael Dell was a true business-model pioneer. The model he created is, by now, well known: While other personal-computer makers sold through resellers, Dell sold directly to end customers. That not only cut out costly link from the value chain, it also gave Dell the information it needed to manage inventory better than any other company in its industry. And because the pace of innovation in the industry was intense, Dell's inventory advantage meant it could avoid the high cost of obsolescence that other computer makers had to bear. Armed with its innovative business model, Dell has consistently outperformed rivals for more than a decade.

In this case, Dell's business model functioned much like a strategy: It made Dell different in ways that were hard to copy. If Dell's rivals tried to sell direct, they would disrupt their existing distribution channels and alienate the resellers on whom they relied. Trapped by their own strategies, they were damned if they copied Dell and damned if they didn't. When a new model changes economics of an industry and is difficult to replicate, it can by itself create a strong competitive advantage.

What often gets lost in Dell's story, though, is the role that pure strategy has played in the company's superior performance. While Dell's direct business model laid out which value chain activities Dell would do (and which it wouldn't do), the company still had crucial strategic choices to make about which customers to serve and what kinds of products and services to offer. In the 1990s for example, while other PC makers focused on computers for the home market, Dell consciously chose to go after large corporate accounts, which were far more profitable. Other PC makers offered low-end machines to lure in first-time buyers. Michael Dell wasn't interested in this "no-margin" business. He staked out his territory selling more powerful, higher margin computers.

Then, because Dell sold direct and could analyze its customers in depth, it began to notice that its average selling price to consumers was increasing while the industry's was falling. Consumers who were buying their second or third machines and who were looking for more power and less hand-holding were coming to Dell—even though it wasn't targeting them. Only in 1997, *after* it had a profitable, billion-dollar consumer business, did Dell dedicate a group to serving the consumer segment.

Now that everyone in its industry is selling direct, Dell's strategy has shifted to deal with the new competitive realities. With a decade-long lead, Dell is by far the industry's best executor of the direct-selling model—it is the low-cost producer. So it is using its cost advantage in PCs to compete on price, to gain share, and to drive the weaker players out of the business. At the same time, the company is relying on its core business model to pursue opportunities in new product markets, like servers, that have greater profit potential than PCs. The underlying business model remains the same. The strategic choices about where to apply the model— which geographic markets, which segments, which customers, which products—are what change.

Clarity about its business model has helped Dell in another way: as a basis for employee communication and motivation. Because a business model tells a good story, it can be used to get everyone in the organization aligned around the kind of value the company wants to create. Stories are easy to grasp and easy to remember. They help individuals to see their own jobs within the larger context of what the company is trying to do and to tailor their behavior accordingly. Used in this way, a good business model can become a powerful tool for improving execution.

Today, "business model" and "strategy" are among the most sloppily used terms in business; they are often stretched to mean everything—and end up meaning nothing. But as the experiences of companies like Dell and Wal-Mart show, these are concepts with enormous practical value. It's true that any attempt to draw sharp boundaries around abstract terms involves some arbitrary choices. But unless we're willing to draw the line somewhere, these concepts will remain confusing and difficult to use. Definition brings clarity. And when it comes to concepts that are so fundamental to performance, no organization can afford fuzzy thinking.

Notes

1. James C. Collins and Jerry I. Porras, *Built to Last* (HarperCollins, 1994).
2. "Meg Whitman at eBay Inc. (A)," HBS case no.9-400-035.
3. "Wal-Mart Stores, Inc.," HBS case no.9-794-024.

JOAN MAGRETTA is a management consultant and a past winner of HBR's McKinsey Award. This article draws on her book *What Management Is* (Free Press, 2002).

Originally published in May 2002. Reprint R0205F

Are You Ignoring Trends That Could Shake Up Your Business?

by Elie Ofek and Luc Wathieu

IT'S HARDLY A REVELATION that digital products and services are playing an increasingly central role in consumers' everyday lives, that the Great Recession has made people more cautious about spending money, and that growing public concern about global warming is influencing purchasing decisions. But are you paying enough attention to the deeper implications of those trends? Are you accounting for the fact that heavy users of digital products and services tend to focus more on short-term goals, demand immediate gratification, expect to multitask, and are open to exchanging ideas with people they've never met in person? Or that the prolonged recession has unleashed not a malaise but rather a desire to be uplifted and energized? Or that green consumers are skeptical of corporations that claim to share their concerns but don't motivate them to act in environmentally friendly ways?

Most managers can articulate the major trends of the day. But in the course of conducting field and market research in a number of industries and working directly with companies, we have discovered that managers often fail to recognize the less obvious but profound ways these trends are influencing consumers' aspirations, attitudes, and behaviors. This is especially true of trends that managers view as peripheral to their core markets.

Consequently, they ignore trends in their innovation strategies, they include product features that only superficially address a trend's impact on consumers, or they adopt a wait-and-see approach and let competitors take the lead. At a minimum, such responses result in missed profit opportunities or wasteful investments in R&D. At the extreme, they can jeopardize a company by ceding to rivals the opportunity to transform the industry. The purpose of this article is twofold: to spur managers to think more expansively about how trends could engender new value propositions in their core markets, and to provide some high-level advice on how to make market research and product development organizations more adept at analyzing and exploiting trends.

The Gold in Trends

At first blush, spending a lot of resources to incorporate elements of a seemingly irrelevant trend into one's core offerings sounds like it's hardly worthwhile. But

Idea in Brief

Virtually all managers in consumer businesses recognize major social, economic, and technological trends. But many do not consider the profound ways in which trends—especially those that seem unrelated to their core markets—influence consumers' aspirations, attitudes, and behaviors. As a result, companies may be ceding to rivals an opportunity to transform the industry. For instance, the impact of the digital revolution on consumers' daily lives is hardly a revelation. But it may be less obvious that heavy digital users tend to focus on short-term goals, demand immediate gratification, and expect to multitask. That insight, the authors argue, is as important for a company that sells lipstick as it is for one that sells smartphones. The authors present a process for identifying the trends that could reshape a business and three strategies for leveraging trends to create new value propositions: Infuse aspects of the trend into the product category to augment traditional offerings, as Coach did with its lower-priced Poppy handbags. Combine aspects of the trend with attributes of the category to produce offerings that transcend it, as Nike did with its Nike+ sports kit and web service. Or counteract negative effects of the trend with new products and services that reaffirm the category's values, as iToys did with its ME2 video game, which encourages children to be physically active.

consider Nike's move to combine its reputation in high-performance athletic footwear with the iPod's meteoric success. In 2006, the company, which accounts for the largest share of running shoes sold in the United States, teamed up with Apple to launch Nike+: a digital sports kit comprising a sensor that attaches to your running shoe and a wireless receiver that connects to your iPod. As you jog and listen to your favorite music, the sensor tracks your speed and distance and the calories you've burned, and transmits that information to your iPod in real time. Back at your computer, you can upload your data to nikeplus.com, which stores your information and provides a user-friendly interface that lets you track your progress.

The kit also allows you to specify a goal and check your performance during your run simply by pressing the iPod's center button. In addition, the website links to social networks like Facebook and Twitter so that you can find and form groups of runners at your level who are interested in sharing challenges and performance information. Nike is now expanding the kit to other athletic activities: It recently launched a version for gym workouts.

So far Nike+ has been a big success. More than 2.5 million kits have been sold, many of them to people who also purchased Nike shoes that have a special recess to house the sensor. Considering that the sports kits retail for about $30 and the shoes for an average of $80, this is no small change.

But the Nike+ story is about much more than the revenues generated from product and accessory sales. What is fascinating is how the new offering catapulted Nike from being relevant to just one aspect of the runner's exercise regime to being at the very center of it. For a Nike+ customer, the Nike brand is no longer about just the product attached to his or her feet; it's about the total exercise experience, including the community.

The Nike+ example represents one of three broad innovation strategies that firms can embrace to address powerful trends. They can *infuse* aspects of the trend into their existing category to *augment* their products or services. They can *combine* aspects of the trend with attributes of their category to produce radical offerings that *transcend* their traditional category and create a new one (as Nike did). Or they can *counteract* negatively perceived effects of the trend by developing products and services that *reaffirm* their category's distinctive values.

Infuse and Augment

The objective of this strategy is to design a new product or service that retains most of the attributes and functions of traditional products in the category but adds others that address the needs and desires unleashed by a major trend. Put simply, this strategy is about augmenting the existing category, not inventing a totally new one. A case in point is the Poppy line of handbags, which Coach created in response to the economic downturn.

By the time the global recession hit Coach's core North American market with full force, late in 2008, the Coach brand had been a symbol of opulence and luxury for nearly 70 years. For $300 to $350, the price of a typical Coach handbag, a woman could signal to the world that she belonged to the elite. The company's consistent execution of this value proposition (through product design, advertising, store layout, and location) fueled a steady rise in sales through much of the past decade. But in the summer of 2008, management had to decide how to respond to the global downturn and the resulting increase in price sensitivity.

The knee-jerk reaction would have been to lower prices on most products and perhaps shift more sales to outlet stores. However, those actions would have risked cheapening the brand's image and eroding the company's meticulously established value proposition. They would have constituted a superficial response to the downturn's likely enduring impact on consumers' expectations and perceptions.

To their credit, Coach's managers did not panic. Instead, they launched a consumer-research project, which revealed that a decreased willingness to spend money was only a small piece of a new mind-set. People had not lost hope or become passive about the future because of economic woes, the gloomy financial outlook, and general uncertainty; on the contrary, they were eager to find ways to lift themselves and the country out of tough times. An attitude of "Yes, we can" had set in. Consumers' desire for status and pampering had not vanished, but the economic reality had created a new layer of needs.

Using these insights, Coach created the lower-priced Poppy line, which it launched in June 2009. The handbags, which sell for about $250, come in vibrant colors and are much more youthful and playful than traditional Coach products. The company's name appears on the bags but is written in graffiti style.

The Poppy line is off to a great start: It helped lift Coach's North American same-store sales by 3.2% in the second quarter of fiscal year 2010, the first increase since the crisis began. Creating the sub-brand allowed Coach to avoid an across-the-board price cut. In contrast to the many companies that responded to the recession by cutting the cost, features, and price of existing products, Coach saw the new consumer mind-set as an opportunity for innovation and renewal.

Another example of the infuse-and-augment strategy is Tesco's response to consumers' growing concerns about the environment. Market research shows that a large proportion of consumers, especially in Europe, have become receptive to the call to save the planet. They want to do their share but are somewhat skeptical of corporations that claim to care about being green. In addition, they often believe that green consumption should lead to a simpler, more economical life.

With that in mind, Tesco, the third-largest retailer in the world, introduced its Greener Living program, which demonstrates the company's commitment to protecting the environment by involving consumers in ways that produce tangible results. For example, Tesco customers can rent company-sponsored plots for gardening and coops for raising egg-laying chickens, and can accumulate points for such activities as reusing bags, recycling cans and printer cartridges, and buying home-insulation materials. Like points earned on regular purchases, these green points can be redeemed for cash. Tesco has not abandoned its traditional retail offerings. Instead, it has augmented its business with these activities, thereby infusing its value proposition with a green streak.

Combine and Transcend

This strategy is more radical than the infuse-and-augment approach. It entails combining aspects of the product's existing value proposition with attributes that address the aspirations, attitudes, and behaviors arising from a trend to create a novel experience—one that may land the company in an entirely new market space.

By combining Nike's original value proposition for amateur athletes with one for digital consumers, the Nike+ sports kit and web interface has moved the company from a focus on athletic apparel to a new plane of engagement with its customers. Yes, shoes are still an essential component of the value proposition, and yes, Nike still caters to many of the same consumer aspirations it always has (the desire to achieve, perform, and win). But Nike+ provides an experience that is as much about managing one's goals in a personalized, efficient, interactive, and real-time fashion as it is about aspiring to be like Michael Jordan or Roger Federer.

Another company that has transcended a traditional category by tapping the digital trend is stickK.com. Americans who want to lose weight spend more than $40 billion a year on pills, diet shakes, books, and programs like Jenny Craig and Weight Watchers. But spending money is relatively easy; the challenge is remaining committed to a regimen. The same is true of programs designed to help people overcome other unhealthy habits, such as smoking and excessive drinking.

The founders of stickK.com—two Yale professors and a student at Yale's School of Management—understood not only the challenge of overcoming bad habits but also that connecting with others and sharing personal thoughts and activities on digital platforms had become the norm. The service they launched in 2008 reflects that insight.

New Value Propositions

Coach's Poppy Collection

Yes, the recession has made consumers more cautious about spending. But after discovering that the downturn has also unleashed a desire to be energized and inspired, Coach created its lower-priced and playful Poppy line of handbags.

Nike+

Nike's insights into how the heavy use of digital products and services was changing consumers' attitudes and behaviors led it to team up with Apple to create the Nike+ sports kit and web service—an offering that transcends Nike's traditional sports apparel category.

iToys' ME2

Canada's iToys addressed parents' concerns that video games were turning their children into couch potatoes by launching the ME2, a handheld game with a pedometer that awards superior virtual skills to kids who get physical exercise.

As a user of stickK.com, you articulate a personal goal (for example, "I will shed one pound every week until I lose 20 pounds") and demonstrate your commitment to it by signing a contract. As you work toward your goal, you post regular entries, which are monitored by a friend or relative you've designated as your referee. The website allows you to create an incentive to fulfill your goal. One option is to form a network of friends who will immediately be notified by e-mail if you violate the terms of your contract. Another is to bet on yourself: You decide on a wager and to whom the money should go if you fail to achieve a milestone. Some people designate a charity or cause that they oppose—a pro-choice or pro-life group, for example, or an institution associated with a political party, such as the Bush or Clinton presidential library. You supply your credit card information through a secure online form, and if you fail to fulfill your contract, the transaction is executed automatically.

As of the start of 2010, stickK.com had nearly 40,000 active contracts and more than $4 million in wagers. Weight loss accounts for nearly 45% of the contracts, but stickK allows individuals to specify any goal—from getting an A on an upcoming exam to "not playing online Scrabble again until the end of the year." The company has ushered in a new era of electronic accountability.

Counteract and Reaffirm

This approach involves developing products or services that emphasize the values traditionally associated with the category in ways that allow consumers to oppose— or at least temporarily escape from—the aspects of trends they view as negative. A product that accomplishes this is the ME2, a handheld video game created by Canada's iToys. By reaffirming the toy category's association with physical play, the ME2 counteracts some of the widely perceived negative impacts of digital gaming devices.

One is the unhealthy lifestyle these devices seem to engender. American fourth-grade boys spend an average of about 10 hours a week playing video and computer games. Many researchers have found that such behavior usually comes at the expense of physical activity and interactions with other children, leading to a host of medical, developmental, and social problems. For example, video games and other digital products have been blamed for contributing to the alarming growth in obesity among children, which has been linked to a sharp rise in diseases such as diabetes and high blood pressure.

The ME2, introduced by iToys in mid-2008, caters to kids' huge desire to play video games while countering the negatives. Like other handheld games, the device features a host of exciting interactive games, a full-color LCD screen, and advanced 3D graphics. What sets it apart is that it incorporates the traditional physical component of children's play: It contains a pedometer, which tracks and awards points for physical activity (walking, running, biking, skateboarding, climbing stairs). The child can use the points to enhance various virtual skills needed for the video game. The more physical activity a child engages in, the greater his or her advantage in the game.

The Current Card, a prepaid debit card for teens, is another example of the power of a counteract-and-reaffirm approach. This new financial tool is Discover's response to the challenge of parenting teenagers in an age when they have much more freedom than they used to, in part because of digital technologies. The card is also the company's attempt to counter two negative aspects of the digital revolution that can spell trouble for teens: the risk of out-of-control shopping, particularly online, and the false sense of expertise that can result from the abundance of information available on the internet.

Teens, like adults, are prone to believe they know more than they actually do about many topics. For example, in a 2008 survey of teens aged 12 to 17, 79% said that they were knowledgeable about basic financial concepts—but the average score of a Federal Reserve Board test of financial literacy given to high school seniors is 48%. This false confidence, combined with the lure of online offerings, can make it very difficult for parents to instill in their children a sense of financial responsibility. Discover has stepped up to this challenge with the Current Card, which lets parents control their children's expenditures (whether online or in bricks-and-mortar stores) by specifying how the card can be used. Through a web interface, parents can track every transaction and receive e-mail notifications if any activity breaks the rules. With this product, Discover not only gives parents a new tool for developing their teens' personal-finance savvy but also reaffirms its core business of facilitating convenient yet responsible spending.

A Four-Step Process for Addressing Trends

To tap a profound consumer trend, you'll need audacity and imagination: audacity to consider that the fight against terrorism might influence computer design, that there could be a lipstick specially suited to the digital age, that the fear of global warming might inspire new kitchenware; and imagination to conceive innovations that compellingly augment, transcend, or reaffirm your existing category. Here is a four-step process that we have successfully applied at a number of companies.

1. Identify Trends That Matter

The obvious first step is identifying the trends, particularly the seemingly peripheral ones, that have the potential to reshape your business. At any point, only a handful of big trends are capable of changing consumers' aspirations, attitudes, and behaviors. Our simple exercise can help you gauge whether certain forces or events constitute a trend worth leveraging. It involves analyzing the following:

Ripple effects. Are changes occurring in multiple areas of a consumer's life? For instance, consider how social networks like Facebook and LinkedIn are affecting both friendships and professional relationships.

Impact. How profound are the changes in people's priorities, perceptions of their role in society, and expectations?

Scope. Does the trend encompass a large number of consumers across market segments?

Endurance. Are there indications that these changes will be a dominant force in consumer behavior for an extended period?

The concern about global warming and the environment is an example of a consumer trend that passes these tests. People try to save paper and electricity at work and at home and look for natural ingredients when deciding which foods, cosmetics, and furniture to purchase. Many firms have made green marketing

Why Firms Fail to Leverage Trends

TRACKING TRENDS IS ONE THING. Making sure your product development group takes them seriously and integrates them appropriately is another. Our research has found that three traps can prevent firms from constructively engaging important consumer trends.

1. Ignoring trends that originate outside their markets. Most firms naturally think of themselves as offering products within defined categories. ("We are an athletic apparel company." "We make cosmetics." "We design luxury handbags.") This often directs innovation efforts toward customer needs that have been considered relevant in the category. Even when firms look for latent or new needs, their aim is often to uncover the shortcomings of existing products—not to come up with new offerings that incorporate consumer behavior from distant areas. The result: They miss out on opportunities presented by trends that seem peripheral. In running shoes, for example, if market research explores only consumers' attitudes about shock absorption, durability, and rapid acceleration, the company will fail to consider how digital behaviors lead to new experiences that transcend the category.

2. Responding to a trend in a superficial way. Trends are widely noticed: They are covered in the media and may directly affect a firm's employees and core customers. This can prompt R&D and marketing professionals to try to respond too quickly—before the

tactics a priority and have appointed corporate sustainability officers. Millions of people have seen Al Gore's movie *An Inconvenient Truth*. The number of people who use multiple recycling bins has increased dramatically. More and more consumers now show up at supermarkets with reusable shopping bags. All these developments indicate that environmental concerns have become deeply embedded and will endure.

company has developed a deep understanding of how the trend is affecting consumers. The result: ill-conceived offerings that don't speak to consumers' new needs or desires and often dilute, rather than enhance, the brand's equity. Consider the flop of Xelibri 6, a smartphone for women created by Siemens that contained two mirrors and was designed like a makeup compact—but could not actually hold makeup. The rise of digital media has prompted consumers to seek products that allow them to multitask, but Siemens didn't appreciate that people expect such products to deliver this benefit in substance, not just in form.

3. Waiting too long. Putting off action can be as risky as responding too quickly. Given the uncertainty about the relevance of a trend and the risks of incorporating it incorrectly, many firms choose to let other firms take the lead in experimenting. Their rationale is that if a competitor comes up with a significant innovation, they can follow quickly. Although a fast-follower strategy sometimes works, it holds dangers. For example, first movers often lock up valuable assets. A case in point: Nike was able to secure a partnership with Apple to cocreate Nike+, a sports kit and web service that allows runners to track their performance with their iPods and share information with others. Given the iPod's popularity among joggers, a firm that now seeks to enter the new space faces an uphill battle.

Identifying trends requires avoiding some common traps (see the sidebar "Why Firms Fail to Leverage Trends") and devoting resources to exploring changes occurring outside one's turf. One option is to create an internal group to do this. Nokia, for example, has an Insight and Foresight team charged with analyzing shifts in consumer tastes not necessarily related to preferences in cell-phone technologies. A firm can also hire a market research or management consulting firm that tracks trends and analyzes their effects (see "The 10 Trends You Have to Watch," HBR July–August 2009).

2. Conduct Two Separate Explorations

The next step involves two completely distinct deep dives. The first is into the less obvious effects of the trend: What important goals, beliefs, and perceptions are emerging among consumers? Are people developing new assumptions about social roles and interactions? The second exploration is of consumers' perceptions and behaviors related to your product category. Various research techniques (open-ended questionnaires, discussion groups, diaries, and interviews of lead users) can help with this analysis.

Consider the case of a beauty-care company that wants to leverage the digital lifestyle trend. A study of heavy users of digital devices might reveal that they expect information about almost anything to be readily available, seek to control and customize experiences, and love to share often mundane events with others in real time. An analysis of the beauty-care category might show that consumers see an imperfection such as a blemish or wrinkle as a weakness and want to associate with products that help them attain socially respected outcomes such as a promotion at work, a higher salary, and prestige.

In conducting this exercise, companies should also probe for undesired outcomes and deficiencies related to the trend and to the existing category. For example, being "always on" and available on social network sites generates strong ambivalent feelings: People struggle between wanting to know what their friends are up to at all times and wanting some privacy. And a consumer who buys beauty-care products often finds it difficult to obtain reliable information about which product is a good match for her skin type; as a result, she might waste money and time experimenting with multiple products.

3. Compare the Results

Once you have a comprehensive understanding of the most important aspects of the consumer trend and of your product category, it is time to envision how key aspects of the trend might relate to key aspects of the consumption experiences in your category. You might discover a great deal of congruence, a disconnect, or perhaps even a latent conflict between your category and the trend you are trying to engage.

For example, a primary goal of beauty-care consumers is enhancing their self-esteem. They might turn to a product to help them look successful, gain the respect of others, and mask their physical flaws. Consumers expect cosmetics brands to deliver products that help them achieve an ideal standard of beauty (often represented by a celebrity or a supermodel) and offer skin-care products to reduce wrinkles and conceal blemishes.

Self-esteem is also a central theme in digital experiences, but it is achieved in entirely different ways in this domain than it is in beauty care. In their digital activities, individuals develop self-esteem by expressing their uniqueness and interacting with others who can appreciate their distinct profiles. Thus, while consumers in both the trend and product-category domains share the goal of self-esteem, there's a disconnect: Beauty-care companies traditionally help them reach ideal standards of beauty, whereas digital tools enable them to cultivate unique profiles.

4. Isolate Potential Strategies

Once you have gained perspective on how important concepts pertaining to your category interact with vital trend-related changes in consumer attitudes and behaviors, you can determine which of our three innovation strategies to pursue. When your category's basic value proposition continues to be meaningful for consumers influenced by the trend, the infuse-and-augment strategy will allow you to reinvigorate the category. If analysis reveals a growing disconnect between your category and consumers' new focus, your innovations need to transcend the category to integrate the two worlds. Finally, if aspects of the category clash with undesired changes emerging from a trend, there is an opportunity to counteract those changes by reaffirming the core values of your category.

Trends—technological, economic, environmental, social, or political—that affect how people perceive the world around them and shape what they expect from products and services present firms with unique opportunities for growth. But firms need to learn how to ride a trend's wave to success. If they don't, they risk being swept away by its powerful tide.

ELIE OFEK is the T.J. Dermot Dunphy Professor of Business Administration at Harvard Business School. **LUC WATHIEU** holds the Ferrero Chair in International Marketing at the European School of Management and Technology in Berlin.

Originally published in July 2010. Reprint R1007M

Creating New Market Space

by W. Chan Kim and Renée Mauborgne

COMPETING HEAD-TO-HEAD can be cutthroat, especially when markets are flat or growing slowly. Managers caught in this kind of competition almost universally say they dislike it and wish they could find a better alternative. They often know instinctively that innovation is the only way they can break free from the pack. But they simply don't know where to begin. Admonitions to develop more creative strategies or to think outside the box are rarely accompanied by practical advice.

For almost a decade, we have researched companies that have created such fundamentally new and superior value. We have looked for patterns in the way companies create new markets and re-create existing ones, and we have found six basic approaches. All come from looking at familiar data from a new perspective; none requires any special vision or foresight about the future.

Most companies focus on matching and beating their rivals, and as a result their strategies tend to converge along the same basic dimensions of competition. Such companies share an implicit set of beliefs about "how we compete in our industry or in our strategic group." They share a conventional wisdom about who their customers are and what they value, and about the scope of products and services their industry should be offering. The more that companies share this conventional wisdom about how they compete, the greater the competitive convergence. As rivals try to outdo one another, they end up competing solely on the basis of incremental improvements in cost or quality or both.

Creating new market space requires a different pattern of strategic thinking. Instead of looking within the accepted boundaries that define how we compete, managers can look systematically across them. By doing so, they can find unoccupied territory that represents a real breakthrough in value. This article will describe how companies can systematically pursue value innovation by looking across the conventionally defined boundaries of competition—across substitute industries, across strategic groups, across buyer groups, across complementary product and service offerings, across the functional-emotional orientation of an industry, and even across time.

Looking Across Substitute Industries

In the broadest sense, a company competes not only with the companies in its own industry but also with companies in those other industries that produce substitute products or services. In making every purchase

Idea in Brief

When the market in which you compete gets overcrowded, innovating is the only way to break free from the pack. But how do you begin? Consider **value innovation**—a strategic concept Kim and Mauborgne introduced in their 1997 *Harvard Business Review* article. Value innovators create products or services for which there are no direct competitors—and use those offerings to stake out and dominate new market spaces. They don't possess special vision or prescience; rather, they look across the conventional boundaries of competition for opportunities to provide breakthrough value for customers.

Take Intuit. In 1984, the software company looked beyond its own industry to identify choices available to consumers seeking to manage their personal finances. Buyers' options? The computer, for which costly, complicated financial management software was available—or the lowly pencil, which didn't simplify things or save time but was cheap and easy to use. Intuit created a third option: the astoundingly successful Quicken software. With its user-friendly interface, basic functions, and affordable price, Quicken leverages the computer's advantages (speed and accuracy) *and* the pencil's advantages (simplicity of use and affordability).

Operating in markets that initially have no rivals, value innovators enjoy steep growth. Consider Starbucks, which transformed a functional product (coffee) into an emotional one with its chain of "caffeine-induced oases" offering chic gathering places, relaxation, and creative coffee drinks. Starbucks enjoys margins roughly five times the industry average.

decision, buyers implicitly weigh substitutes, often unconsciously. Going into town for dinner and a show? At some level, you've probably decided whether to drive, take the train, or call a taxi. The thought process is intuitive for individual consumers and industrial buyers alike.

For some reason, however, we often abandon this intuitive thinking when we become sellers. Rarely do

Idea in Practice

To spot additional value innovation opportunities, consider these approaches.

Look across strategic groups. Strategic groups are clusters of companies within an industry that all pursue a similar strategy, such as offering low prices or a glamorous image for consumers. Most companies try to enhance their competitive position *within* a strategic group. To create a new market space, identify factors that determine buyers' decisions to trade up or down from one group to another.

> *Example:* Sony created a whole new market: personal portable stereos. Its Walkman combined the virtues of products created by two strategic groups: manufacturers of boom

boxes, characterized by great acoustics and "cool" image, and makers of transistor radios, valued for their low prices and convenient size and weight. The Walkman grabbed market share from the two strategic groups, and attracted new groups of customers, such as joggers and commuters.

Look across the chain of buyers. Instead of targeting a single obvious customer group, target other customers involved in the buying decision. Overlooked buyer groups value different features than target customers, suggesting fresh innovation opportunities.

> *Example:* While other online financial-information providers served brokerage IT managers, Bloomberg

sellers think consciously about how their customers make trade-offs across substitute industries. A shift in price, a change in model, even a new ad campaign can elicit a tremendous response from rivals within an industry, but the same actions in a substitute industry usually go unnoticed. Trade journals, trade shows, and consumer rating reports reinforce the vertical walls that stand between one industry and another. Often, however, the space between substitute industries provides opportunities for value innovation.

began serving traders and analysts. Bloomberg designed a system to offer these neglected buyers tools for accessing and immediately acting on financial information. The system included keyboards labeled with familiar financial terms, press-of-a-button analytic capability, and dual monitors for multitasking. The system also improved the quality of traders' personal lives—providing purchasing services that enabled overworked traders to buy flowers, clothing, and jewelry during trading lulls that occurred during the workday.

Look across complementary products and services. Seek untapped value hidden in other industries' offerings that affect *your* offerings' value. Define the total solution buyers seek when choosing a product or service—including what they do before, during, and after using your product.

> *Example:* With their blockbuster superstores, Borders Books & Music and Barnes & Noble transformed their product from *books* to *the pleasure of reading.* Coffee bars, wide aisles, and comfy armchairs invite people to linger. Book-savvy staff help customers make selections. And late-night closing times provide evenings of quiet reading away from harried home fronts.

Consider Home Depot, the company that has revolutionized the do-it-yourself market in North America. In 20 years, Home Depot has become a $24 billion business, creating over 130,000 new jobs in more than 660 stores. By the end of the year 2000, the company expects to have over 1,100 stores in the Americas. Home Depot did not achieve that level of growth simply by taking market share away from other hardware stores; rather, it has created a new market of do-it-yourselfers out of ordinary home owners.

There are many explanations for Home Depot's success: its warehouse format, its relatively low-cost store locations, its knowledgeable service, its combination of large stores and low prices generating high volumes and economies of scale. But such explanations miss the more fundamental question: Where did Home Depot get its original insight into how to revolutionize and expand its market?

Home Depot looked at the existing industries serving home improvement needs. It saw that people had two choices: they could hire contractors, or they could buy tools and materials from a hardware store and do the work themselves. The key to Home Depot's original insight was understanding why buyers would choose one substitute over another. (It is essential here to keep the analysis at the industry, and not the company, level.)

Why do people hire a contractor? Surely not because they value having a stranger in their house who will charge them top dollar. Surely not because they enjoy taking time off from work to wait for the contractor to show up. In fact, professional contractors have only one decisive advantage: they have specialized know-how that the home owner lacks.

So executives at Home Depot have made it their mission to bolster the competence and confidence of customers whose expertise in home repair is limited. They recruit sales assistants with significant trade experience, often former carpenters or painters. These assistants are trained to walk customers through any project—installing kitchen cabinets, for example, or building a deck. In addition, Home Depot sponsors in-store clinics that teach customers such skills as electrical wiring, carpentry, and plumbing.

To understand the rest of the Home Depot formula, now consider the flip side: Why do people choose hardware stores over professional contractors? The most common answer would be to save money. Most people can do without the features that add cost to the typical hardware store. They don't need the city locations, the neighborly service, or the nice display shelves. So Home Depot has eliminated those costly features, employing a self-service warehouse format that lowers overhead and maintenance costs, generates economies of scale in purchasing, and minimizes stock-outs.

Essentially, Home Depot offers the expertise of professional home contractors at markedly lower prices than hardware stores. By delivering the decisive advantages of both substitute industries—and eliminating or reducing everything else—Home Depot has transformed enormous latent demand for home improvement into real demand.

Intuit, the company that changed the way individuals and small businesses manage their finances, also got its insight into value innovation by thinking about how customers make trade-offs across substitutes. Its Quicken software allows individuals to organize, understand, and manage their personal finances. Every household goes through the monthly drudgery of paying bills. Hence, in principle, personal financial software should be a big and broad market. Yet before Quicken, few people used software to automate this tedious and repetitive task. At the time of Quicken's release in 1984, the 42 existing software packages for personal finance had yet to crack the market.

Why? As Intuit founder Scott Cook recalls, "The greatest competitor we saw was not in the industry. It was the pencil. The pencil is a really tough and resilient substitute. Yet the entire industry had overlooked it."

Asking why buyers trade across substitutes led Intuit to an important insight: the pencil had two decisive advantages over computerized solutions—amazingly low cost and extreme simplicity of use. At prices of around $300, existing software packages were too expensive. They were also hard to use, presenting intimidating interfaces full of accounting terminology.

Intuit focused on bringing out both the decisive advantages that the computer has over the pencil—speed and accuracy—and the decisive advantages that the pencil has over computers—simplicity of use and low price—and eliminated or reduced everything else. With its user-friendly interface that resembles the familiar checkbook, Quicken is far faster and more accurate than the pencil, yet almost as simple to use. Intuit eliminated the accounting jargon and all the sophisticated features that were part of the industry's conventional wisdom about "how we compete." It offered instead only the few basic functions that most customers use. Simplifying the software cut costs. Quicken retailed at about $90, a 70% price drop. Neither the pencil nor other software packages could compete with Quicken's divergent value curve. Quicken created breakthrough value and re-created the industry, and has expanded the market some 100-fold. (See the exhibit "Creating a new value curve.")

There is a further lesson to be drawn from the way Intuit thought about and looked across substitutes. In looking for other products or services that could perform the same function as its own, Intuit could have focused on private accounting firms that handle finances for individuals. But when there is more than one substitute, it is smart to explore the ones with the greatest volumes in usage as well as in dollar value. Framed that way, more Americans use pencils than accountants to manage their personal finances.

Many of the well-known success stories of the past decade have followed this path of looking across substitutes to create new markets. Consider Federal Express and United Parcel Service, which deliver mail at close to the speed of the telephone, and Southwest Airlines, which combines the speed of flying with the convenience of frequent departures and the low cost of driving. Note that Southwest Airlines concentrated on driving as the relevant substitute, not other surface transportation such as buses, because only a minority of Americans travels long distances by bus.

Looking Across Strategic Groups Within Industries

Just as new market space often can be found by looking across substitute industries, so can it be found by looking across *strategic groups*. The term refers to a group of companies within an industry that pursue a similar

Creating a new value curve

The value curve—a graphic depiction of the way a company or an industry configures its offering to customers—is a powerful tool for creating new market space. It is drawn by plotting the performance of the offering relative to other alternatives along the key success factors that define competition in the industry or category.

To identify those alternatives, Intuit, for example, looked within its own industry—software to manage personal finances—and it also looked across substitute products to understand why customers chose one over the other. The dominant substitute for software was the lowly pencil. The value curves for these two alternatives map out the existing competitive space.

The value curves in personal finance before Quicken

The software offered relatively high levels of speed and accuracy. But customers often chose the pencil because of its advantages in price and ease of use, and most customers never used the software's optional features, which added cost and complexity to the product.

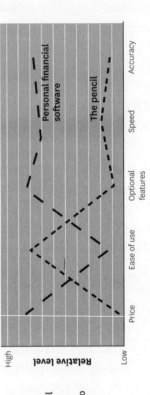

Key elements of product, service, and delivery

The key to discovering a new value curve lies in asking four basic questions.

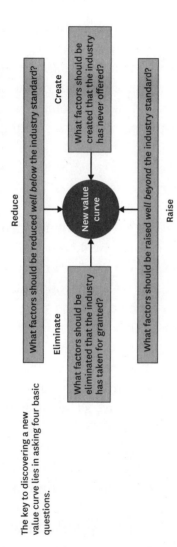

Eliminate

What factors should be eliminated that the industry has taken for granted?

Reduce

What factors should be reduced well *below* the industry standard?

New value curve

Create

What factors should be created that the industry has never offered?

Raise

What factors should be raised well *beyond* the industry standard?

Quicken's value curve

Answering the four questions led Intuit to create a new value curve, which combines the low price and ease of use of the pencil with the speed and accuracy of traditional personal-financial software.

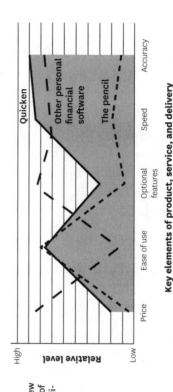

Key elements of product, service, and delivery

strategy. In most industries, all the fundamental strategic differences among industry players are captured by a small number of strategic groups.

Strategic groups can generally be ranked in a rough hierarchical order built on two dimensions, price and performance. Each jump in price tends to bring a corresponding jump in some dimension of performance. Most companies focus on improving their competitive position *within* a strategic group. The key to creating new market space across existing strategic groups is to understand what factors determine buyers' decisions to trade up or down from one group to another.

Consider Polo Ralph Lauren, which created an entirely new and paradoxical market in clothing: high fashion with no fashion. With worldwide retail sales exceeding $5 billion, Ralph Lauren is the first American design house to successfully take its brand worldwide.

At Polo Ralph Lauren's inception more than 30 years ago, fashion industry experts of almost every stripe criticized the company. Where, they asked, was the fashion? Lacking creativity in design, how could Ralph Lauren charge such high prices? Yet the same people who criticized the company bought its clothes, as did affluent people everywhere. Lauren's lack of fashion was its greatest strength. Ralph Lauren built on the decisive advantages of the two strategic groups that dominated the high-end clothing market—designer haute couture and the higher-volume, but lower-priced, classical lines of Burberry's, Brooks Brothers, Aquascutum, and the like.

What makes people trade either up or down between haute couture and the classic lines? Most customers don't trade up to haute couture to get frivolous fashions that are rapidly outdated. Nor do they enjoy paying ridiculous prices that can reach $500 for a T-shirt. They buy haute couture for the emotional value of wearing an exclusive designer's name, a name that says, "I am different; I appreciate the finer things in life." They also value the wonderfully luxurious feel of the materials and the fine craftsmanship of the garments.

The trendy designs the fashion houses work so hard to create are, ironically, the major drawback of haute couture for most high-end customers, few of whom have the sophistication or the bodies to wear such original clothing. Conversely, customers who trade down for classic lines over haute couture want to buy garments of lasting quality that justifies high prices.

Ralph Lauren has built its brand in the space between these two strategic groups, but it didn't do so by taking the average of the groups' differences. Instead, Lauren captured the advantages of trading both up and down. Its designer name, the elegance of its stores, and the luxury of its materials capture what most customers value in haute couture; its updated classical look and price capture the best of the classical lines. By combining the most attractive factors of both groups, and eliminating or reducing everything else, Polo Ralph Lauren not only captured share from both segments but also drew many new customers into the market.

Many companies have found new market space by looking across strategic groups. In the luxury car market, Toyota's Lexus carved out a new space by offering the quality of the high-end Mercedes, BMW, and Jaguar at a price closer to the lower-end Cadillac and Lincoln. And think of the Sony Walkman. By combining the acoustics and the "cool" image of boom boxes with the low price and the convenient size and weight of transistor radios, Sony created the personal portable-stereo market in the late 1970s. The Walkman took share from these two strategic groups. In addition, its quantum leap in value drew into the market new customers like joggers and commuters.

Michigan-based Champion Enterprises found a similar opportunity by looking across two strategic groups in the housing industry: makers of prefabricated housing and on-site developers. Prefabricated houses are cheap and quick to build, but they are also dismally standardized and project an image of low quality. Houses built by developers on-site offer variety and an image of high quality but are dramatically more expensive and take longer to build.

Champion created new market space by offering the decisive advantages of both strategic groups. Its prefabricated houses are quick to build and benefit from tremendous economies of scale and lower costs, but Champion also allows buyers to choose such high-end options as fireplaces, skylights, and even vaulted ceilings. In essence, Champion has changed the definition of prefabricated housing. As a result, far more lower-to-middle-income consumers have become interested in purchasing prefabricated housing rather than renting or buying an apartment, and even some affluent people are being drawn into the market.

Looking Across the Chain of Buyers

In most industries, competitors converge around a common definition of who the target customer is when in reality there is a chain of "customers" who are directly or indirectly involved in the buying decision. The *purchasers* who pay for the product or service may differ from the actual *users,* and in some cases there are important *influencers,* as well. While these three groups may overlap, they often differ.

When they do, they frequently hold different definitions of value. A corporate purchasing agent, for example, may be more concerned with costs than the corporate user, who is likely to be far more concerned with ease of use. Likewise, a retailer may value a manufacturer's just-in-time stock-replenishment and innovative financing. But consumer purchasers, although strongly influenced by the channel, do not value these things.

Individual companies in an industry often target different customer segments—large versus small customers, for example. But an industry typically converges on a single buyer group. The pharmaceutical industry, for example, focuses overridingly on influencers—the doctors. The office equipment industry focuses heavily on purchasers—corporate purchasing departments. And the clothing industry sells predominantly to users. Sometimes there is a strong economic rationale for this focus. But often it is the result of industry practices that have never been questioned.

Challenging an industry's conventional wisdom about which buyer group to target can lead to the discovery of new market space. By looking across buyer groups, companies can gain new insights into how to redesign their value curves to focus on a previously overlooked set of customers.

Consider Bloomberg. In little over a decade, Bloomberg has become one of the largest and most profitable business-information providers in the world. Until Bloomberg's debut in the early 1980s, Reuters and Telerate dominated the on-line financial-information industry, providing news and prices in real time to the brokerage and investment community. The industry focused on purchasers—the IT managers—who valued standardized systems, which made their lives easier.

This made no sense to Bloomberg. Traders and analysts, not IT managers, make or lose millions of dollars for their employers each day. Profit opportunities come from disparities in information. When markets are active, traders and analysts must make rapid decisions. Every second counts.

So Bloomberg designed a system specifically to offer traders better value, one with easy-to-use terminals and keyboards labeled with familiar financial terms. The systems also have two flat-panel monitors, so traders can see all the information they need at once without having to open and close numerous windows. Since traders have to analyze information before they act, Bloomberg added a built-in analytic capability that works with the press of a button. Before, traders and analysts had to download data and use a pencil and calculator to perform important financial calculations. Now users can quickly run "what if" scenarios to compute returns on alternative investments, and they can perform longitudinal analyses of historical data.

By focusing on users, Bloomberg was also able to see the paradox of traders' and analysts' personal lives. They have tremendous income but work such long hours that they have little time to spend it. Realizing that markets have slow times during the day when little trading takes place, Bloomberg decided to add information and purchasing services aimed at enhancing traders' personal lives. Traders can buy items like flowers, clothing, and jewelry; make travel arrangements; get information about wines; or search through real estate listings.

By shifting its focus upstream from purchasers to users, Bloomberg created a value curve that was radically different from anything the industry had ever seen. The traders and analysts wielded their power within their firms to force IT managers to purchase Bloomberg terminals. Bloomberg did not simply win customers away from competitors—it grew the market. "We are in a business that need not be either-or," explains founder Mike Bloomberg. "Our customers can afford to have two products. Many of them take other financial news services and us because we offer uncommon value." (See the graph "Bloomberg's value curve at its debut.")

Philips Lighting Company, the North American division of the Dutch company Philips Electronics, re-created its industrial lighting business by shifting downstream from purchasers to influencers. Traditionally, the industry focused on corporate purchasing

Bloomberg's value curve at its debut

To establish its value curve, Bloomberg looked across the chain of buyers from the IT managers that had traditionally purchased financial information systems to the traders who used them. Its value innovation stemmed from a combination of creating new features—such as on-line analytic capabilities—that traders rather than IT managers value and raising ease of use by an order of magnitude.

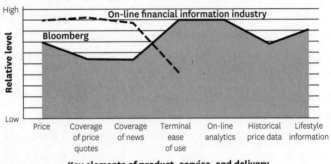

managers who bought on the basis of how much the lightbulbs cost and how long they lasted. Everyone in the industry competed head-to-head along those two dimensions.

By focusing on influencers, including CFOs and public relations people, Philips came to understand that the price and life of bulbs did not account for the full cost of lighting. Because lamps contained environmentally toxic mercury, companies faced high disposal costs at the end of a lamp's life. The purchasing department never saw those costs, but CFOs did. So in 1995, Philips introduced the Alto, an environmentally friendly bulb that it promotes to CFOs and to public relations people, using those influencers to drive sales. The Alto reduced customers' overall costs and garnered companies positive press for promoting environmental concerns. The new market Alto created has superior margins and is growing rapidly; the product has already replaced more than 25% of traditional T-12 fluorescent lamps used in stores, schools, and office buildings in the United States.

Many industries afford similar opportunities to create new market space. By questioning conventional definitions of who can and should be the target customer, companies can often see fundamentally new ways to create value.

Looking Across Complementary Product and Service Offerings

Few products and services are used in a vacuum; in most cases, other products and services affect their value. But in most industries, rivals converge within the bounds of their industry's product and service offerings. Take movie theaters as an example. The ease and cost of getting a babysitter and parking the car affect the perceived value of going to the movies, although these complementary services are beyond the bounds of the movie theater industry as it has been traditionally defined. Few cinema operators worry about how hard or costly it is for people to get babysitters. But they should, because it affects demand for their business.

Untapped value is often hidden in complementary products and services. The key is to define the total solution buyers seek when they choose a product or service. A simple way to do so is to think about what happens before, during, and after your product is used. Babysitting and parking the car are needed before going to the movies. Operating and application software are used along with computer hardware. In the airline industry, ground transportation is used after the flight but is clearly part of what the customer needs to travel from one place to another.

Companies can create new market space by zeroing in on the complements that detract from the value of their own product or service. Look at Borders Books & Music and Barnes & Noble in the United States. By the late 1980s, the U.S. retail-book industry appeared to be in decline. Americans were reading less and less. The large chains of mall bookstores were engaged in intense competition, and the small, independent bookstore appeared to be an endangered species.

Against this backdrop, Borders and B&N created a new format—book superstores—and woke up an entire industry. When either company enters a market, the overall consumption of books often increases by more than 50%.

The traditional business of a bookstore had been narrowly defined as selling books. People came, they bought, they left. Borders and B&N, however, thought more broadly about the total experience people seek when they buy books—and what they focused on was the joy of lifelong learning and discovery. Yes, that involves the physical purchase of books. But it also includes related activities: searching and hunting, evaluating potential purchases, and actually sampling books.

Traditional retail-book chains imposed tremendous inefficiencies and inconveniences on consumers. Their staffs were generally trained as cashiers and stock clerks; few could help customers find the right book. In small stores, selection was limited, frustrating the search for an exciting title. People who hadn't read a good book review recently or picked up a recommendation from a friend would be unlikely to patronize these bookstores. As a rule, the stores discouraged browsing, forcing customers to assume a large part of the risk in buying a book, since people would not know until after they bought it whether they would like it. As for consumption, that activity was supposed to occur at home. But as people's lives have become increasingly harried, home has become less likely to be a peaceful oasis where a person can enjoy a wonderful book.

Borders and B&N saw value trapped in these complementary activities. They hired staff with extensive knowledge of books to help customers make selections. Many staff members have college or even advanced degrees, and all are passionate book lovers. Furthermore, they're given a monthly book allowance, and they're actually encouraged to read whenever business is slow.

The superstores stock more than 150,000 titles, whereas the average bookstore contains around 20,000. The superstores are furnished with armchairs, reading tables, and sofas to encourage people not just to dip into a book or two but to read them through. Their coffee bars, classical music, and wide aisles invite people to linger comfortably. They stay open until 11 at night, offering a relaxing destination for an evening of quiet

Value innovation in book retailing

Borders and Barnes & Noble looked across complementary products and services to establish a new value curve in book retailing. Their book superstores raised the selection of books, the level of staff knowledge, and the range of store hours well above the industry standards while lowering price and creating a wholly new reading environment.

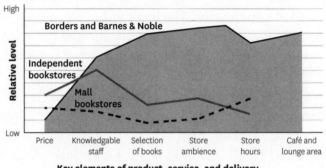

reading, not a quick shopping stop. (See the graph "Value innovation in book retailing.")

Book superstores redefined the scope of the service they offer. They transformed the product from the book itself into the pleasure of reading and intellectual exploration. In less than six years, Borders and B&N have emerged as the two largest bookstore chains in the United States, with a total of more than 650 superstores between them.

We could cite many other examples of companies that have followed this path to creating new market space. Virgin Entertainment's stores combine CDs, videos, computer games, and stereo and audio equipment to satisfy buyers' complete entertainment needs.

Dyson designs its vacuum cleaners to obliterate the costly and annoying activities of buying and changing vacuum cleaner bags. Zeneca's Salick cancer centers combine all the cancer treatments their patients might need under one roof so they don't have to go from one specialized center to another, making separate appointments for each service they require.

Looking Across Functional or Emotional Appeal to Buyers

Competition in an industry tends to converge not only around an accepted notion of the scope of its products and services but also around one of two possible bases of appeal. Some industries compete principally on price and function based largely on calculations of utility; their appeal is rational. Other industries compete largely on feelings; their appeal is emotional.

Yet the appeal of most products or services is rarely intrinsically one or the other. The phenomenon is a result of the way companies have competed in the past, which has unconsciously educated consumers on what to expect. Companies' behavior affects customers' expectations in a reinforcing cycle. Over time, functionally oriented industries become more functionally oriented; emotionally oriented industries become more emotionally oriented. No wonder market research rarely reveals new insights into what customers really want. Industries have trained customers in what to expect. When surveyed, they echo back: more of the same for less.

Companies often find new market space when they are willing to challenge the functional-emotional orientation of their industry. We have observed two common patterns. Emotionally oriented industries offer many extras that add price without enhancing functionality. Stripping those extras away may create a fundamentally simpler, lower-priced, lower-cost business model that customers would welcome. Conversely, functionally oriented industries can often infuse commodity products with new life by adding a dose of emotion—and in so doing, can stimulate new demand.

Look at how Starbucks transformed a functional product into an emotional one. In the late 1980s, General Foods, Nestlé, and Procter & Gamble dominated the U.S. coffee market. Consumers drank coffee as part of a daily routine. Coffee was considered a commodity industry, marked by heavy price-cutting and an ongoing battle for market share. The industry had taught customers to shop based on price, discount coupons, and brand names that are expensive for companies to build. The result was paper-thin profit margins and low growth.

Instead of viewing coffee as a functional product, Starbucks set out to make coffee an emotional experience, what customers often refer to as a "caffeine-induced oasis." The big three sold a commodity—coffee by the can; Starbucks sold a retailing concept—the coffee bar. The coffee bars offered a chic gathering place, status, relaxation, conversation, and creative coffee drinks. Starbucks turned coffee into an emotional experience and ordinary people into coffee connoisseurs for whom the steep $3-per-cup price seemed reasonable. With almost no advertising, Starbucks became a national brand with margins roughly five times the industry average.

What Starbucks did for coffee, Swatch did for budget watches. Long considered a functional item, budget watches were bought merely to keep track of time. Citizen and Seiko, the leaders in the industry, competed through advances in functionality by using quartz technology to improve accuracy, for example, or by making digital displays that were easier to read. Swatch turned budget watches into fashion accessories.

SMH, the Swiss parent company, created a design lab in Italy to turn its watches into a fashion statement, combining powerful technology with fantasy. "You wear a watch on your wrist, right against your skin," explains chairman Nicholas Hayek. "It can be an important part of your image. I believed that if we could add genuine emotion to the product and a strong message, we could succeed in dominating the industry and creating a powerful market." Before Swatch, people usually purchased only one watch. Swatch made repeat purchases the standard. In Italy, the average person owns six Swatches to fit their different moods and looks.

The Body Shop created new market space by shifting in the opposite direction, from an emotional appeal to a functional one. Few industries are more emotionally oriented than cosmetics. The industry sells glamour and beauty, hopes and dreams as much as it sells products. On average, packaging and advertising constitute 85% of cosmetics companies' costs.

By stripping away the emotional appeal, the Body Shop realized tremendous cost savings. Since customers get no practical value from the money the industry spends on packaging, the Body Shop uses simple refillable plastic bottles. The Body Shop spends little on advertising, again because its customers get no functional value from it. In short, the Body Shop hardly looks like a cosmetics company at all. The company's approach—and its emphasis on natural ingredients and healthy living—was so refreshingly simple that it won consumers over through common sense and created new market space in an industry accustomed to competing on a tried-and-true formula. (See the graph "Is the Body Shop a cosmetics company?")

Is the Body Shop a cosmetics company?

By reconsidering the traditional basis of appeal of its industry, the Body Shop created a value curve so divergent that it hardly looks like a cosmetics company at all. In appealing to function rather than emotion, the Body Shop reduced price, glamour, and packaging costs while creating a new emphasis on natural ingredients and healthy living.

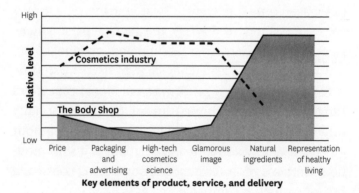

A burst of new market creation is under way in a number of service industries that are following this pattern. Relationship businesses like insurance, banking, and investing have relied heavily on the emotional bond between broker and client. They are ripe for change. Direct Line Insurance in Britain, for example, has done away with traditional brokers. It reasoned that customers would not need the hand-holding and emotional comfort that brokers traditionally provide if the company did a better job of, for example, paying claims rapidly and eliminating complicated paperwork. So instead of using brokers and regional branch offices, Direct Line substitutes information technology to improve claims handling, and it passes on some of the cost savings to customers in the form of lower insurance premiums. In the United States, Vanguard Group in index funds and Charles Schwab in brokerage services are doing the same in the investment industry, creating new market space by transforming emotionally oriented businesses based on personal relationships into high-performance, low-cost functional businesses.

Looking Across Time

All industries are subject to external trends that affect their businesses over time. Think of the rapid rise of the Internet or the global movement toward protecting the environment. Looking at these trends with the right perspective can unlock innovation that creates new market space.

Most companies adapt incrementally and somewhat passively as events unfold. Whether it's the emergence of new technologies or major regulatory changes, managers tend to focus on projecting the trend itself. That is, they ask in which direction a technology will evolve, how it will be adopted, whether it will become scalable. They pace their own actions to keep up with the development of the trends they're tracking.

But key insights into new market spaces rarely come from projecting the trend itself. Instead they arise from business insights into how the trend will change value to customers. By looking across time—from the value a market delivers today to the value it might deliver tomorrow—managers can actively shape their future and lay claim to new market space. Looking across time is perhaps more difficult than the previous approaches we've discussed, but it can be made subject to the same disciplined approach. We're not talking about predicting the future, which is inherently impossible. We're talking about finding insight in trends that are observable today. (See the diagram "Shifting the focus of strategy.")

Three principles are critical to assessing trends across time. To form the basis of a new value curve, these trends must be decisive to your business, they must be irreversible, and they must have a clear trajectory. Many trends can be observed at any one time—a discontinuity in technology, the rise of a new lifestyle, or a change in regulatory or social environments, for example. But usually only one or two will have a decisive impact on any particular business. And it may be

Shifting the focus of strategy

From head-to-head competition to creating new market space

The conventional boundaries of competition	Head-to-head competition	Creating new market space
Industry	focuses on rivals within its industry	looks across substitute industries
Strategic group	focuses on competitive position within strategic group	looks across strategic groups within its industry
Buyer group	focuses on better serving the buyer group	redefines the buyer group of the industry
Scope of product and service offerings	focuses on maximizing the value of product and service offerings within the bounds of its industry	looks across to complementary product and service offerings that go beyond the bounds of its industry
Functional-emotional orientation of an industry	focuses on improving price-performance in line with the functional-emotional orientation of its industry	rethinks the functional-emotional orientation of its industry
Time	focuses on adapting to external trends as they occur	participates in shaping external trends over time

possible to see a trend or major event without being able to predict its direction. In 1998, for example, the mounting Asian crisis was an important trend certain to have a big impact on financial services. But the direction that trend would take was impossible to predict—and therefore envisioning a new value curve that might result from it would have been a risky enterprise. In contrast, the euro is evolving along a constant trajectory as it replaces Europe's multiple currencies. This is a decisive, irreversible, and clearly developing trend upon which new market space might be created in financial services.

Having identified a trend of this nature, managers can then look across time and ask themselves what the market would look like if the trend were taken to its logical conclusion. Working back from that vision of a new value curve, they can then identify what must be changed today to unlock superior value for buyers.

Consider Enron, an energy company based in Houston, Texas. In the 1980s, Enron's business centered on gas pipelines. Deregulation of the gas industry was on the horizon. Such an event would certainly be decisive for Enron. The U.S. government had just deregulated the telecom and transportation industries, so a reversal in its intent to deregulate the gas industry was highly unlikely. Not only was the trend irreversible, its logical conclusion was also predictable—the end of price controls and the breakup of local gas monopolies. By assessing the gap between the market as it stood and the market as it was to be, Enron gained insight into how to create new market space.

When local gas monopolies were broken up, gas could be purchased from anywhere in the nation. At the time, the cost of gas varied dramatically from region to region. Gas was much more expensive, for example, in New York and Chicago than it was in Oregon and Idaho. Enron saw that deregulation would make possible a national market in which gas could be bought where it was cheap and sold where it was expensive. By examining how the gas market could operate with deregulation, Enron saw a way to unlock tremendous trapped value on a national scale.

Accordingly, Enron worked with government agencies to push for deregulation. It purchased regional gas-pipeline companies across the nation, tied them together, and created a national market for gas. That allowed Enron to buy the lowest cost gas from numerous sources across North America and to operate with the best spreads in the industry. Enron became the largest transporter of natural gas in North America, and its customers benefited from more reliable delivery and a drop in costs of as much as 40%.

Cisco Systems created a new market space in a similar way. It started with a decisive and irreversible trend that had a clear trajectory: the growing demand for high-speed data exchange. Cisco looked at the world as it was—and that world was hampered by slow data rates and incompatible computer networks. Demand was exploding as, among other factors, the number of Internet users doubled roughly every 100 days. So Cisco could clearly see that the problem would inevitably worsen. Cisco's routers, switches, and other networking devices were designed to create breakthrough value for customers, offering fast data exchanges in a seamless networking environment. Thus Cisco's insight is as much about value innovation as it is about technology. Today more than 80% of all traffic on the Internet flows through Cisco's products, and its margins in this new market space are in the 60% range.

Regenerating Large Companies

Creating new market space is critical not just for start-ups but also for the prosperity and survival of even the world's largest companies. Take Toyota as an example. Within three years of its launch in 1989, the Lexus accounted for nearly one-third of Toyota's operating profit while representing only 2% of its unit volume. Moreover, the Lexus boosted Toyota's brand image across its entire range of cars. Or think of Sony. The greatest contribution to Sony's profitable growth and its reputation in the last 20 years was the Walkman. Since its introduction in 1979, the Walkman has dominated the personal portable-stereo market, generating a huge positive spillover effect on Sony's other lines of business throughout the world.

Likewise, think of SMH. Its collection of watch companies ranges from Blancpain, whose watches retail for over $200,000, to Omega, the watch of astronauts, to midrange classics like Hamilton and Tissot to the sporty, chic watches of Longines and Rado. Yet it was the creation of the Swatch and the market of fun, fashionable watches that revitalized the entire Swiss watch industry and made SMH the darling of investors and customers the world over.

It is no wonder that corporate leaders throughout the world see market creation as a central strategic challenge to their organizations in the upcoming decade. They understand that in an overcrowded and demand-starved economy, profitable growth is not sustainable without creating, and re-creating, markets. That is what allows small companies to become big and what allows big companies to regenerate themselves.

W. CHAN KIM is the Boston Consulting Group Bruce D. Henderson Chaired Professor of Strategy and International Management at Insead in France. **RENÉE MAUBORGNE** is a professor of strategy and management at Insead.

Originally published in January 1999. Reprint 99105

Building Breakthrough Businesses Within Established Organizations

by Vijay Govindarajan and Chris Trimble

FEW BUSINESS NARRATIVES are more evocative than that of the inspired leader boldly pursuing an extraordinarily innovative idea. So romantic is the notion that companies pushing for more innovation often devote the bulk of their energies and resources to generating ideas and encouraging individual initiatives. This is a good start, but nothing more. New businesses with the potential to deliver breakthrough growth for established companies face stiff headwinds well after launch. Ray Stata, a cofounder of Analog Devices, the $2 billion semiconductor company, has lived this challenge for decades: "I came to the conclusion long ago that limits to innovation have less to do with technology or creativity than organizational agility. Inspired individuals can only do so much." Emphasis must shift: from ideas to execution and from leadership excellence to organizational excellence.

To find out exactly what it takes to get beyond ideas, we have spent the past five years chronicling initiatives at organizations such as the New York Times Company, Analog Devices, Corning, Hasbro, Cisco, Unilever, Kodak, Johnson & Johnson, Nucor, Stora Enso, and the Thomson Corporation. We have examined best practices for managing strategic experiments—high-growth-potential new businesses that depart from an organization's current business model and that target emerging industries in which no clear formula exists for making a profit. Strategic experiments constitute the highest-risk, highest-return category of innovation and require a unique managerial approach. We chose to focus on strategic experiments because dramatic forces such as globalization, digital technology, biotechnology, and demographic change are now creating nonlinear shifts in the economy—threatening stability but also opening up opportunities for breakthrough growth.

A new business with high growth potential (let's call it NewCo) rarely coexists gracefully with the most closely related established business unit within the company (let's call it CoreCo). The unnatural combination creates three specific challenges for NewCo: *forgetting, borrowing,* and *learning.* NewCo must forget some of what made CoreCo successful, because NewCo and CoreCo have elemental differences. NewCo must borrow some of CoreCo's assets—the greatest advantage it has over

Idea in Brief

Why did toy and gaming giant Hasbro unload its new software division at a rock-bottom price just five years after launching it? Like many other established companies, Hasbro learned the hard way that new ventures rarely coexist peacefully with the core businesses that launched them. The company failed to nurture its nascent division—and the venture stumbled badly.

Innovative ideas aren't enough to fuel breakthrough growth in a new business. To thrive, new ventures must surmount three challenges:

- Forget some of what has made your core business successful—such as which skills to acquire and which customers to serve.

- Borrow only those assets from your core business—

brands, sales relationships, manufacturing capacity—that provide a distinct competitive advantage.

- Learn quickly. The faster you resolve your venture's inevitable unknowns, the sooner you'll zero in on a winning business model.

To master these challenges, you must redesign virtually every aspect of your new business—from hiring, performance evaluation, and budgeting to compensation, definitions of success, and reporting relationships. Hard work? Yes. But the payoff is worth it. By artfully blending forgetting, borrowing, and learning, the New York Times Company's new Internet division turned around a dismal start and generated profits just a few years after launch.

independent start-ups. And NewCo must be prepared to learn some things from scratch.

When Analog Devices decided to explore opportunities presented by a new semiconductor technology, it faced all three challenges. The technology, called microelectromechanical systems (MEMS), uses a chip with microscopic moving parts that act as sensors; the first commercial application was automotive crash

Idea in Practice

To translate breakthrough business ideas into breakthrough growth.

Forget

Your new venture has unique answers to the questions "Who's our customer?" "What value do we offer?" and "How do we deliver that value?" Yet institutional memory (stories about the established company's history, or traditional performance measures) can prevent the new business's leaders from forgetting the old answers. Your strategy? Restructure the nascent division.

> ***Example:*** Corning launched Corning Microarray Technologies (CMT) to make glass laboratory apparatus for the emerging genomics industry. CMT stumbled initially, after adopting Corning's traditional product-development

model—which didn't apply to genomics work. Only after Corning restructured CMT did the division launch a successful product. Changes included appointing a new general manager, who facilitated communication between businesspeople and scientists and consolidated far-flung CMT employees to develop a unique culture.

Borrow

Borrow assets from your core business *only* if they afford such a competitive advantage that you'd highlight it in a pitch to outside investors. Typically just one or two areas (e.g., Corning's expertise in glass manufacturing) will meet this criterion. Once you've borrowed, manage the resulting tensions between your new and old businesses.

sensors, which launch airbags. The MEMS team at Analog Devices needed to *forget,* because the company's core business model wouldn't work for MEMS. Analog Devices was accustomed to serving thousands of customers with thousands of products, many designed for custom applications. There were only a few automakers, however, and because they valued cost and reliability

Example: When the New York Times Company's Internet business, New York Times Digital (NYTD), borrowed the newspaper's branded content and advertiser base, an "us versus them" undertone developed. The paper's editorial staff worried about protecting its brand; its circulation department accused the Internet business (which offered free content) of cannibalizing newspaper subscriptions.

To manage the tension, company leaders conducted analyses showing that the Web site was *generating* new newspaper subscriptions. And during performance reviews, managers stressed the importance of cross-unit collaboration. Results? After becoming profitable, NYTD began generating $30 million-plus annually on revenues of $100 million.

Learn

By analyzing disparities between your new business's predicted and actual performance, you can develop a winning business model or exit a hopeless situation in time. Expect that early predictions will be wild guesses. Resist the temptation to discard them: In time, your guesses become informed estimates and then reliable forecasts.

To accelerate learning, create and review simple business plans at frequent intervals. Evaluate your new division's and core business's performance in separate meetings. Don't judge performance of the nascent unit's leader against standards used in the old business. Instead, evaluate his or her ability to learn and make good decisions.

over customization, they needed only a few variations on the basic crash sensor. As a result, the MEMS team had to alter all of its processes for selling, marketing, and manufacturing. The team also needed to *borrow* Analog Devices' semiconductor expertise and manufacturing plants. And it needed to *learn* whether MEMS devices could be manufactured at a profit and to what extent markets for MEMS applications outside the automotive industry would develop. The business ultimately became profitable but not without first having to confront each of the three challenges.

Forgetting, borrowing, and learning are monumental tasks. That's why it's crucial for a company to leverage the power of organizational design—a term we use in its broadest sense. In building NewCo, the CEO must be willing to challenge the status quo on an extraordinary range of issues: hiring, individual performance evaluation, needed competencies, reporting relationships, decision rights, planning and budgeting, business performance assessment, metrics, compensation, shared values, and shared assumptions about success.

The three challenges are present throughout NewCo's awkward adolescence, from launch to profitability. And they're present all at once, which means tackling them requires an understanding of how they're related. Forgetting and borrowing are at odds, for example, and need to be balanced. A sole focus on forgetting would suggest isolation of NewCo, while a sole focus on borrowing would suggest full integration of NewCo. Also, failure to forget cripples the learning effort. If NewCo cannot leave behind CoreCo's formula for success, it will not find its own.

Forget

To build a foundation for success, NewCo must forget CoreCo's business model. NewCo's answers to the fundamental questions that define a business—Who is our customer? What value do we offer? How do we deliver that value?—should be different from CoreCo's. NewCo must therefore leave behind notions about what skills and competencies are most valuable. And it must forget the relative predictability of CoreCo's environment.

It is easy to underestimate the magnitude of the forgetting challenge. And it is easy to conclude too quickly that NewCo has succeeded in forgetting. Awareness of the differences between NewCo and CoreCo is not enough. Forgetting is about changing behavior. Often, we have observed, NewCo talks like NewCo but acts like CoreCo.

Many powerful sources of institutional memory—instincts developed through past experiences, relationships between employees that are grounded in CoreCo's business model, performance measures, planning templates, norms for individual performance evaluation, and even often-told stories about the company's history—can interfere with forgetting. Some companies have especially strong memories. (See the sidebar "Warning Signs That Forgetting Will Be an Uphill Battle.")

Many firms make the mistake of duplicating CoreCo's organizational design when they create NewCo. Doing so minimizes hassles, since making NewCo an exception to rules about such things as hiring, compensation, and status can lead to resistance, even resentment, within CoreCo. But the only way to erase memory is to overhaul NewCo's organizational design.

To understand what it takes to forget, consider Corning's venture into the genomics industry. Through the 1990s, advances in biotechnology spawned an industry

Warning Signs That Forgetting Will Be an Uphill Battle

- The company has only one business model.

- All business units within the company are at similar points in the business life cycle (starting up, rapidly growing, steadily expanding, maturing, or declining).

- CoreCo has well-established standards of business performance that do not apply to NewCo—often because NewCo has a different cost structure.

- The company has a well-defined culture and has effective socialization mechanisms built into its hiring and acquisition processes.

- The company has a history of promoting primarily from within.

- The company has a strong culture of holding people accountable to plans.

---

dedicated to serving the needs of genomics researchers, who were trying to unlock the secrets of DNA and unleash a revolution in medical therapies. Millions of new experiments became possible, and researchers desperately wanted to automate and accelerate the experimentation process.

One crucial piece of laboratory apparatus was the DNA microarray—a glass slide with thousands of tiny DNA samples adhered to it. Because of issues of quality, reliability, and ease of use, many researchers "printed" their own microarrays—a time-consuming and costly process. The opportunity for Corning was clear: to leverage its world-class expertise in specialty glass and microscopic manufacturing processes so it could offer genomics researchers a reliable and inexpensive supply of microarrays. When Corning launched Corning Microarray Technologies (CMT) in 1998, analysts were projecting explosive growth for the industry.

Over the years, Corning had been effective in part because its business units shared a common formula for success. Each sold components to industrial manufacturers. Each emphasized high quality and reliability. Each depended on strong intellectual property rights that limited competition. Each relied on excellence in the manufacture of glass and ceramics and on mastery of related scientific fields. Each planned in a disciplined fashion, and each held managers accountable to those plans.

But CMT was different. CMT sold to an unfamiliar customer—senior laboratory administrators. It needed to emphasize cost and convenience instead of the highest possible quality. It had to work in an unfamiliar, emerging scientific field where patent protection was unlikely. It needed to balance expertise in glass manufacturing with expertise in molecular biology. And it faced a much higher level of ambiguity.

The differences between Corning and CMT are clear in hindsight. But at the time, Corning naturally assumed that what had worked for its established business units would also work for CMT. Therefore, CMT had its own manufacturing, sales, and marketing functions and shared Corning's centralized research and development functions. CMT also adopted Corning's rigorous five-stage model for new product development, along with clear expectations for hitting certain milestones. Because

CMT was small, it reported to the existing life sciences business unit. Corning did depart from its tradition of hiring and promoting from within—CMT hired several outside experts in molecular biology, many of whom were assigned to the centralized R&D groups—but all management positions were filled by Corning insiders. As a result, CMT did not develop a culture or identity that was noticeably different from Corning's.

Nonetheless, within months, CMT achieved its first success. It offered researchers who printed their own microarrays a much-improved *un*printed glass slide (without DNA adhered to it) with a special coating. Customers were thrilled with the improved consistency they achieved in printing their own microarrays.

Ambitions for CMT escalated. Its leaders thought that if they simply stuck to the plan, breakthrough growth and profitability would certainly follow. But CMT soon faced unanticipated difficulties.

Working with DNA presented unfamiliar challenges. DNA from different suppliers had chemical inconsistencies, and Corning's usual methods for identifying and correcting manufacturing problems were confounded by the peculiarities of DNA fluid. One day the process would appear to be working fine; the next day a mysterious new problem would arise.

Soon CMT started missing deadlines established in the business plan. The leadership team felt intense pressure. Corning held managers accountable to the plan. Falling short was failing. Plus, falling behind meant that CMT would drag down the profitability of Corning's life sciences unit, which was just as concerned about hitting its numbers. Rather than reexamine fundamental choices, which would have meant admitting failure and asking for more capital, CMT leaders viewed their struggles as minor setbacks, and they urged their team to work harder.

Despite the high level of urgency, CMT was unable to meet expectations. In an environment of perceived failure, the cohesiveness of the leadership group frayed. The team often settled disagreements by reverting to what had worked in the past. Antagonism also developed between the molecular biology experts that CMT had hired from outside Corning and the CMT leadership team. The molecular biologists took issue with the way the leadership team allocated resources and evaluated outcomes. The biologists also disagreed with decisions to delay product launches to achieve quality standards they knew to be unnecessary in the imperfect world of biotechnology.

All of CMT's struggles stemmed from failures to forget. And all were probably inevitable from the moment CMT adopted Corning's organizational design.

Two years into CMT's operations, turnover in Corning's senior staff led to a reevaluation. Corning's leaders decided to rebuild the CMT organization. First, they appointed a new general manager, someone who had the ability to manage in ambiguous contexts and had a knack for facilitating communication between businesspeople, engineers, and scientists. Second, they reduced the extent to which CMT was integrated with the existing research and development functions by having CMT's heads of R&D report to CMT's general manager. Third, they changed to more subjective criteria for evaluating the general manager's performance, focusing on factors such as how quickly he learned and made adjustments. Fourth, the general manager no longer reported to the head of the life sciences business but to the president of Corning Technologies, who would dedicate significant time and energy to advising CMT.

CMT's new general manager subsequently made his own changes. He hired an outside molecular biology expert to manage the product development effort and another to manage relationships with suppliers. He also moved numerous CMT employees working in distant Corning facilities back to Corning, New York, to help CMT develop a distinct culture.

All of these changes took several months, but it was time well spent. CMT was able to restructure its relationships between research, development, marketing, and sales and to follow a more iterative innovation process. The molecular biologists were given a stronger voice and were able to help CMT make more rapid technical progress. And Corning's senior management team treated CMT's projections as though they were informed estimates rather than a nonnegotiable basis for judging performance. Knowing that he would be evaluated on how quickly he learned and made adjustments, CMT's general manager frequently updated the president on setbacks, lessons, and new directions. When CMT launched its first microarray product in September 2000, customers rated the product a "home run."

How to Forget

From studying Corning's experience—and comparing it to similar efforts at other companies—we have isolated a number of best practices for forgetting:

Don't be insular. NewCo should hire outsiders in key management roles and strongly consider an outsider to head the business. Outsiders challenge institutional memory and are instrumental in building new competencies.

Don't assign status based on size. NewCo should report at least one level above CoreCo in order to reduce the pressures on NewCo for short-term results and to ensure that CoreCo does not hoard resources.

Rearrange the moving parts. NewCo should reconsider how major business functions such as marketing and product development interact. Established patterns of interaction within CoreCo are usually incompatible with the new business model.

Build a new dashboard. The company should not base NewCo's performance on CoreCo's metrics. Doing so reinforces CoreCo's formula for success, not NewCo's.

Dare to make complex judgments. The company should not judge the performance of NewCo's leader too heavily against plans.

Promote new thinking about success. NewCo's leader should create a unique set of beliefs about actions that lead to success and regularly reinforce them. CoreCo's beliefs may not apply in NewCo's environment.

Borrow

NewCo forgets most easily if it is isolated from CoreCo. But complete separation is impractical. CoreCo's tremendous resources are too valuable to ignore.

NewCo *could* borrow a lot from CoreCo—everything from unique assets such as a brand, a network of sales relationships, and manufacturing capacity, to more routine items such as hiring policies, accounting systems, and purchasing processes. We suggest a more measured approach. Borrow too much, and it becomes too hard to forget.

NewCo should borrow when it can gain a crucial competitive advantage—crucial enough that the company would highlight it in a pitch to outside investors. Corning, for example, could not credibly talk to shareholders about its investment in CMT without directing attention to its existing expertise in glass manufacturing. That's a sign that Corning's expertise in glass manufacturing is something CMT should borrow. Usually, there are only one or two such areas that meet this criteria. Incremental cost reductions are never sufficient justification for borrowing.

Links between NewCo and CoreCo should be selected carefully because if NewCo has been properly designed to forget, interactions will be difficult to manage. In fact, once the links are in place, the crux of the borrowing challenge then becomes anticipating the tensions between NewCo and CoreCo—and never allowing them to escalate beyond productive levels. Managing these interactions deserves substantial attention from senior management. Otherwise, cooperation between NewCo and CoreCo can easily disintegrate.

The story of the New York Times Company's venture into the interactive world demonstrates the difficulties of borrowing. The company launched its Internet business unit, eventually named New York Times Digital (NYTD), in 1995. At first, Internet operations were kept closely integrated with newspaper operations. The Internet team prepared content by altering headlines, adding hyperlinks, resizing photos, changing captions, and so forth, keeping the Web site up-to-date throughout the night until the final edition went to press. NYTD added many new features in the early years, but it soon started lagging behind competitors, which were more fully utilizing the rapidly expanding capability of the Internet. Though the NYTD staff pushed to keep pace, it felt constrained to a simple "newspaper.com" operation.

Soon, the company decided on a complete organizational overhaul, choosing an approach similar to Corning's. The head of NYTD began reporting directly to the president rather than to the general manager of the *Times*. NYTD's managers created their own policy team, including a CFO and heads of human resources and business development. They hired so many outsiders with Internet experience that, by the end of 2000, only one-fourth of the staff had come through internal transfers. They altered planning norms and focused on different measures of performance. They moved to a separate building. And they made an effort to redefine their culture and values.

An explosion of creativity followed. The NYTD employees were now operating under the assumption that they served a different set of readers and advertisers than the *Times* and met distinct needs. They experimented with potential revenue sources and added a great deal of content that was not in the daily newspaper, including material from other news sources, audio and video content, interactive features, continuous news breaks, and *Times* archives.

Unfortunately, the organizational overhaul that enabled NYTD to forget also hindered its borrowing. Tensions heightened in the daily interactions between NYTD and the *Times*. And borrowing was absolutely crucial. NYTD needed two links in particular to the *Times*. Most obvious, NYTD could not survive without the newspaper's branded content, the main attraction for its readers. And NYTD needed to tap into the newspaper's existing base of advertisers, which required the coordination of sales processes.

Some tensions arose from substantive business conflicts. For example, the *Times* circulation department, quite understandably, was not enamored with NYTD. Making newspaper content available on the Internet at no charge gave people a powerful reason not to subscribe to the print version of the newspaper. Also, the *Times* editorial staff was concerned about protecting the newspaper's brand. NYTD was primarily a software operation and, as such, was designed to encourage cross-functional collaboration, something strictly limited within the newspaper to ensure that journalism was not influenced by commercial pressures. Finally, the *Times* group that sold display advertisements (as opposed to classifieds) viewed coordination with the NYTD sales team as a distraction, since the *Times* print ads were much bigger sources of revenue.

Tensions rooted in rivalry were also disruptive. NYTD received a great deal of media attention, especially when the company proposed, though never launched, a NYTD tracking stock that would have given NYTD employees a chance at a large payoff. And because NYTD had made it so clear that it was trying to build a different kind of organization, interactions took on an "us versus them" undertone. NYTD communicated that it aimed to be fast moving, antibureaucratic, risk taking, and experimental. Naturally, the *Times* aspired to be the same and winced at the implication that it was not.

These tensions are hardly unique. They are an inevitable part of the challenge of managing strategic experiments. We observed similar tensions in every company we studied. (For more on these tensions, see the sidebar "Warning Signs That Borrowing Will Be an Uphill Battle.")

Whereas other companies in our research struggled to create effective cooperation, the New York Times Company succeeded because the senior management team acknowledged and proactively managed the tensions.

Warning Signs That Borrowing Will Be an Uphill Battle

- CoreCo perceives that NewCo will cannibalize CoreCo revenues.

- CoreCo perceives that NewCo could render a CoreCo competence obsolete.

- CoreCo perceives that NewCo might damage CoreCo assets, such as brands or customer relationships.

- NewCo's losses are rising, even as its leaders are succeeding in growing revenues, and CoreCo managers are questioning the wisdom of allocating capital to a business incurring a loss. Bonuses tied to corporate profits exacerbate the situation.

- Resources are scarce or becoming scarcer as CoreCo goes through a downturn. CoreCo is resistant to allocating capital, manufacturing capacity, employee time, and other resources for NewCo.

- CoreCo managers are unfamiliar with the varying needs of units at different stages in the business life cycle, such as the need to evaluate business performance differently, the need to place more emphasis on flexibility than on efficiency, and the need to hire, promote, and compensate based on unique criteria. In fact, if NewCo managers receive large bonuses

---

The president, in particular, closely monitored interactions between NYTD and the *Times* and intervened when necessary to keep interactions productive.

In addition, in performance reviews of individual managers, the company stressed collaborating across business units. And to minimize tensions over subscription cannibalization, the senior management team conducted an analysis showing that cannibalization was minimal and that the Web site was actually generating

when NewCo succeeds, CoreCo may specifically resent the fact that NewCo's success was dependent upon CoreCo resources.

- Establishing trust between CoreCo and NewCo, two very different organizations, is proving difficult.

- CoreCo managers are jealous of NewCo. This is likely if NewCo starts to receive strong public endorsements from analysts, the press, outside consultants, or the CEO. CoreCo managers have worked for years or decades to advance within CoreCo, and now CoreCo may appear inferior to a much younger and sexier division.

- Stereotypes persist about the capabilities of new and old companies. NewCo may assume that big companies cannot be agile or entrepreneurial, and CoreCo may insist that status should be based solely on resources under command. Such attitudes rarely constitute healthy rivalry—and they can easily disrupt cooperation.

- CoreCo is so disciplined about process efficiency that it refuses to alter any processes on NewCo's behalf.

new subscriptions by inducing trial use of the product online.

In most cases, the company empowered NYTD in its interactions with the *Times*. For example, to help NYTD establish a clear price in the market, the senior management team prohibited any initiative on the part of the *Times* to give away Web advertising as part of a larger print advertising package. (Editorial was one area where the company didn't empower NYTD. To protect the

Times brand, the newspaper retained substantial control over alterations to editorial content on the Web site.)

NYTD reached profitability in 2001, in part because company leaders carefully managed interactions between NYTD and the *Times*. By 2004, NYTD was earning more than $30 million annually on revenues of approximately $100 million.

How to Borrow

Ultimately, NewCo has a much better chance of success when it can leverage CoreCo's assets. The trick, however, is borrowing only where the leverage is highest and ensuring that the senior management team is engaged in monitoring and facilitating. By comparing the New York Times' approach to those of other companies we studied, we were able to identify a number of best practices for borrowing:

> **Balance the yin of forgetting with the yang of borrowing.** Create links, yes, but only to lend NewCo a crucial competitive advantage. Avoid links where conflicts are severe. Avoid links to the IT or HR departments.

> **Find common ground.** Reinforce values that NewCo and CoreCo share. In most cases, CoreCo will have some values that are inconsistent with NewCo's business model. Still, the senior management team can facilitate cooperation by creating a "metaculture" composed of more general values.

Be careful what you ask for. To promote collaboration, reconsider individual incentives. Evaluate and reward CoreCo managers, in part, according to their willingness to cooperate with NewCo. Avoid strong incentives tied strictly to CoreCo's short-term performance.

Co-opt CoreCo. To eliminate resistance from CoreCo's general manager, make borrowing as painless as possible so that he can focus strictly on CoreCo. Replenish CoreCo's resources when NewCo borrows heavily. Set transfer prices high enough to ensure that CoreCo will consider it a priority to help NewCo but not so high that NewCo cannot realistically achieve profitability. NewCo's profitability is a powerful symbol. CoreCo will always be more enthusiastic about helping when there is evidence that NewCo is succeeding.

Be alert to tremors. Assign a senior executive to anticipate tensions between NewCo and CoreCo and to intervene should those tensions become destructive. The senior executive must be willing to commit a lot of time and energy and must be influential and respected within the corporation. She must continually explain the rationale for the differences between NewCo and CoreCo.

Force authority uphill. Unless NewCo is in danger of damaging one of CoreCo's assets, particularly a brand, empower NewCo in its interactions with CoreCo. Without intervention, power will naturally shift back to the larger, more entrenched CoreCo.

Learn

Strategic experiments are highly uncertain endeavors. Regardless of the level of prior research and analysis, NewCo will face several critical unknowns. The faster it can resolve these unknowns—that is, the faster it learns—the sooner it will zero in on a winning business model or exit a hopeless situation.

Any new business has a great deal to learn—new skills to hone, new processes to perfect, new relationships to master. These are important. But the fundamental uncertainties in the business model itself will make or break the business. NewCo's leaders can resolve the critical unknowns most quickly by focusing on a specific task: learning to predict NewCo's business outcomes. At the outset, predictions are always wild guesses. It is not uncommon for revenue forecasts for three years out to be off by a factor of ten. But as the management team learns, wild guesses become informed estimates, and informed estimates become reliable forecasts. (See the exhibit "Is NewCo learning?")

Because predictions are bound to be wrong, especially early on, it is tempting to put little effort into them or quickly discard them. This is a trap. You cannot get better at making predictions by avoiding them. Predictions are important not because of their accuracy but

Is NewCo learning?

Reliable forecasts are the best indicators that a new business is learning.

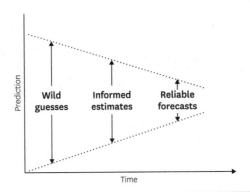

because of the learning opportunities they present. In fact, the crucial learning step for NewCo is analyzing disparities between predictions and outcomes. This analysis must be open and candid. And it must be conducted with speed, rigor, and discipline.

The learning challenge is the most difficult of the three. (See the sidebar "Warning Signs That Learning Will Be an Uphill Battle.") In fact, none of the companies we studied implemented a robust learning process that led to the quick resolution of critical unknowns. Thus, in our field research, we learned much more about what can go wrong than what can go right. The story of Hasbro Interactive illustrates several of the possible pitfalls associated with learning.

In 1995, Hasbro's traditional game business, with iconic brands such as Scrabble and Monopoly, was

Warning Signs That Learning Will Be an Uphill Battle

- NewCo's leader perceives that NewCo is in a tremendous rush to get to market first—and therefore has little time for planning.

- The company has a tradition of very detailed and exact planning.

- The company has a history of insisting on common planning approaches for every business unit.

- Data on NewCo's performance (other than financials) are difficult to gather or highly ambiguous.

- The nature of NewCo's business is such that it demands major onetime commitments and thus has little opportunity to change direction.

- The company strongly penalizes managers who fail to make their numbers.

- One or more measures of business performance are viewed as important throughout the company. Senior executives judge NewCo by the same measures, even though the measures are probably irrelevant to NewCo.

under threat. The ubiquitous PC, with its rapidly expanding multimedia capabilities, appeared to be the future of gaming. Viewing the threat as an opportunity, Hasbro created Hasbro Interactive. With a distinct organizational design and limited links to the core business, Hasbro Interactive succeeded both in forgetting and borrowing. But it would soon struggle with learning.

Hasbro Interactive's initial strategy was conservative. Executives there focused on converting existing

Hasbro products to an interactive format. The new products were a quick success, generating $80 million in revenues and earning a profit in 1997. Hasbro touted Hasbro Interactive's potential to Wall Street analysts.

The division planned to double revenues in 1998. But to get there, Hasbro Interactive would have to pursue much more experimental possibilities. At this point, learning became even more important. Starting in early 1998, Hasbro Interactive bought licenses to produce games based on television shows. They purchased old video game properties, hoping to resurrect classics from the 1980s. They created deals with sports franchises. They acquired other video game producers. They expanded the video game platforms to serve more than just PCs. They began developing their own titles from scratch. And they invested heavily in a new Internet platform, Games.com.

Overall, the heightened ambition was consistent with the anything-is-possible atmosphere of the late 1990s. But the way that Hasbro Interactive pursued growth brought a tremendous number of additional unknowns into the business. For example, did Hasbro Interactive have the skills to develop products from scratch? Could it turn other companies' products into video games as successfully as its own? How quickly would video game players migrate to the Internet? Hasbro Interactive needed an effective learning process to quickly resolve these and other unknowns. Instead, it kept moving ahead aggressively for as long as possible.

Results were strong once again in 1998. Consequently, even though many of the new initiatives had yet to prove themselves, Hasbro Interactive set an audacious target: $1 billion in revenues within three years. The goal was initially just conversational, but it affected decision making and fueled ambition.

Nobody could know it at the time, but as the goal of reaching $1 billion coalesced, Hasbro Interactive entered a new period in its history—the beginning of the end. Results in the first quarter of 1999 were disappointing because of unexpectedly high returns of unsold product from retailers after the 1998 Christmas season. Senior executives at Hasbro became more alert. They had many questions. Concerns heightened when Hasbro Interactive reported a significant loss at the end of 1999—in the tens of millions of dollars. The pressure was on, and it only got worse when Hasbro's core business suffered a slight decline in 2000.

Hasbro Interactive was unable to quickly restore profitability. It had invested a great deal in experimental opportunities and did not want to abandon them before they had a realistic chance to succeed. The end came late in 2000, when turnover in Hasbro's senior management team led to a change in sentiment. The new team would not endure additional losses, and Hasbro Interactive was sold at a disappointing price.

Had Hasbro Interactive been engaged in a learning process from the beginning, a more favorable outcome would have been likely. The business would have been able to part with the specific initiatives that were failing, and it could have continued to build on those that were succeeding. But Hasbro Interactive did not learn quickly because its predictions were not treated with care. They were ignored, they were manipulated, and they became too rigid.

For a variety of reasons, Hasbro Interactive *ignored* its own predictions. First, it dismissed the importance of making them, believing they would be wrong anyway. Its executives felt they were in an all-out race for first-mover advantage and should be focused on doing, not planning. Second, like most companies, Hasbro's planning cycle was annual. But the planning cycle is also the learning cycle. Thus, Hasbro Interactive ignored the fundamental assumptions underlying predictions throughout the year, and learning slowed to a crawl. A quarterly or even monthly frequency would have been a better match for Hasbro Interactive's fast-changing business.

Managers of Hasbro's established toy and game business *manipulated* Hasbro Interactive's predictions by imposing their own performance measures. Starting in 1999, Hasbro held monthly meetings to review the performance of all Hasbro business units. Naturally, the instinct was to evaluate Hasbro Interactive just like any other Hasbro division. For example, Hasbro placed heavy emphasis on short-term profitability—an unrealistic measure, given Hasbro Interactive's risky initiatives. And when Hasbro Interactive's returns from the retail trade were excessive by toy and game standards, it looked bad—even though the terms of trade are very different in software. Finally, when Hasbro Interactive argued that its product development expenses could be capitalized rather than expensed, a practice common in the software industry, others became uncomfortable because the practice was unfamiliar in toys and games. Thus, the measures that shaped the perceived performance of Hasbro Interactive were not those that could help resolve critical unknowns.

Hasbro Interactive also made the mistake of letting its predictions become *too rigid*. For years, Hasbro had applied relatively forgiving standards of accountability to plans because of the inherent unpredictability of the toy business. At the prodding of a senior executive hired from the outside, however, Hasbro had stiffened its standards, which made it unlikely that predictions for Hasbro Interactive could be revised.

Leaders of potentially high-growth businesses often view themselves as bold visionaries, and this also can interfere with the necessary revision of predictions. When it became clear that 1999 revenues would fall short, Hasbro Interactive's leader reaffirmed his belief in the original plan. He insisted on staying the course and continued to promote the $1 billion goal.

CEOs can also inadvertently make predictions inflexible. They may speak loudly of a new business's potential—as Hasbro's top executives did—both to insiders and outsiders. The intent may be to get investors excited, or it may be to increase CoreCo's support for NewCo. But doing so can lock in an overly aggressive prediction. The voice of the CEO is extremely powerful, and expectations can stick.

Rigid predictions, especially long-term ones, often lead to "guardrail-to-guardrail" decision making—that is, aggressive investment followed by complete abandonment. Such a pattern is the opposite of the gradual zeroing-in pattern that marks a healthy learning process. Hasbro Interactive went guardrail to guardrail in large part because of its heavy focus on the $1 billion revenue goal. Tensions escalated as time went by, and people's ability to rationally assess the situation became almost impossible. In the end, those who never believed that $1 billion was feasible managed to drown out the voices of those who saw the potential in Hasbro Interactive—and Hasbro Interactive was abandoned altogether.

How to Learn

Learning is the most difficult of the three challenges. It requires stepping away from tried-and-true, disciplined, and rigorous approaches to planning and moving to something very different but just as disciplined and rigorous. To promote effective learning:

Don't try to mix oil and water. Hold separate meetings for evaluating the business performance of NewCo and CoreCo. These meetings must be handled very differently, and combining them can be impractical, if not destructive.

Protect predictions. Ensure that executives involved in NewCo's planning process understand the importance of improving predictions and are aware of how this learning process can go astray when predictions are ignored, are manipulated, or become rigid.

Avoid being defensive. Evaluate the leader of NewCo not on results but on his ability to learn and make good decisions. Though accountability to plans is an effective practice in mature businesses, it can be crippling in new high-potential businesses. If NewCo's leader is held accountable to the business plan, he will become defensive once targets are missed—a highly likely outcome in any strategic experiment. He will have a hard time being open and candid and may even hide information, perhaps even taking the senior management team out of the learning process altogether.

Do less, faster. That is, simplify plans, but plan more often. Each cycle through the planning process creates a learning opportunity, so planning more frequently increases the learning rate. To make a higher frequency practical, plans must be simplified. Detailed plans (broken down by region, product line, sales channel, and so forth) are useful for mature businesses, but NewCo should focus on resolving critical unknowns, which can be accomplished at a more aggregate level.

Analyze through a new lens. Compare predicted and actual *trends*. Because strategic experiments are dynamic, rates of change are often more valuable information than current results.

Measure what you don't know. Identify metrics that are most useful in resolving critical unknowns.

These are usually nonfinancial measures and are rarely the most closely watched metrics at CoreCo.

———————

Opportunities to lead strategic experiments do not come along every day. In fact, we have encountered very few managers who have led such experiments more than once. Strategic experiments are adventures, and they are challenging—perhaps the "triple flip with a quadruple twist" of general management.

Thus, it is imperative that companies try to learn from others' experiences. The central lesson of history is this: To convert breakthrough ideas into breakthrough growth, you must forget, borrow, and learn. Each has straightforward principles.

Today's executives celebrate an innovation myth focused on gifted visionaries. But the capabilities of the organizations that surround these visionaries will make or break the visions.

VIJAY GOVINDARAJAN is the Earl C. Daum 1924 Professor of International Business and **CHRIS TRIMBLE** is an adjunct associate professor of business administration at Dartmouth's Tuck School of Business. They are the authors of *Ten Rules for Strategic Innovators: From Idea to Execution* (Harvard Business Review Press, 2005), from which this article is adapted.

Originally published in May 2005. Reprint R0505C

Finding Your Next Core Business

by Chris Zook

IT IS A WONDER HOW MANY management teams fail to exploit, or even perceive, the full potential of the basic businesses they are in. Company after company prematurely abandons its core in the pursuit of some hot market or sexy new idea, only to see the error of its ways—often when it's too late to reverse course. Bausch & Lomb is a classic example. Its eagerness to move beyond contact lenses took it into dental products, skin care, and even hearing aids in the 1990s. Today B&L has divested itself of all those businesses at a loss, and is scrambling in the category it once dominated (where Johnson & Johnson now leads). And yet it's also true that no core endures forever. Sticking with an eroding core for too long, as Polaroid did, can be just as devastating. Both these companies were once darlings of Wall Street, each with an intelligent management team and a formerly dominant core. And in a sense, they made the same mistake: They misjudged the point their core business had reached in its life cycle and whether it was time to stay focused, expand, or move on.

How do you know when your core needs to change in some fundamental way? And how do you determine what the new core should be? These are the questions that have driven my conversations with senior managers and the efforts of my research team over the past three years. What we've discovered is that it is possible to measure the vitality remaining in a business's core—to see whether that core is truly exhausted or still has legs. We've also concluded from an in-depth study of companies that have redefined their cores (including Apple, IBM, De Beers, PerkinElmer, and 21 others) that there is a right way to go about reinvention. The surest route is not to venture far afield but to mine new value close to home; assets already in hand but peripheral to the core offer up the richest new cores.

This article discusses both these findings. It identifies the warning signs that a business is losing its potency and offers a way to diagnose the strength remaining in its core. It recounts the efforts of managers in a variety of settings who saw the writing on the wall and succeeded in transforming their companies. And, based on these and other cases, it maps the likely spots in a business where the makings of a new core might be found.

When It's Time for Deep Strategic Change

Not every company that falls on hard times needs to rethink its core strategy. On the contrary, declining performance in what was a thriving business can usually be

Idea in Brief

It's hard to know when your core business must change. Some companies cling too long to their cores, even in the face of crushing competition. Others, lured by hot new markets, abandon their core prematurely—with devastating results.

There *is* a smarter approach, says Zook. First, recognize when it's *truly* time to find a new core. For example, perhaps your growth formula no longer works because your target market is saturated. Then, examine your company's **hidden assets**—neglected businesses, unexplored customer insights, latent capabilities. Ask how they can help you define a new core that will propel fresh growth. For instance, American Express transformed its ailing core charge-card business after discovering neglected data showing how different customer segments used the cards and what other products might interest them.

By redefining your core at the right time *and* in the right way, you boost the odds of profiting from change—before rivals do.

chalked up to an execution shortfall. But when a strategy does turn out to be exhausted, it's generally for one of three reasons.

The first has to do with *profit pools*—the places along the total value chain of an industry where attractive profits are earned. If your company is targeting a shrinking or shifting profit pool, improving your ability to execute can accomplish only so much. Consider the position of Apple, whose share of the market for personal computers plummeted from 9% in 1995 to less than 3% in 2005. But more to the point, the entire profit pool in PCs steadily contracted during those years. If Apple had not moved its business toward digital music, its prospects might not look very bright. General Dynamics was in a similar situation in the 1990s, when

Idea in Practice

Zook offers these guidelines for deciding when it's time to redefine your core business.

Assess the Need for Change

Periodically ask whether your current strategy is exhausted. It may be if:

- **Your company is targeting a shrinking profit pool.** For example, Apple wisely moved toward digital music as the PC profit pool contracted.

- **A new rival has entered the field unburdened by your cost structure.** Compaq, for instance, suffered from Dell's superior economics.

- **Your growth formula isn't sustainable.** For example, a mining firm loses its natural advantage as its mines become depleted.

Recognize the Makings of a New Core

If your business *is* losing potency, remake your core gradually.

Example: Dometic had long sold absorption refrigerators, which have no moving parts and no need for electricity, to boat and recreational-vehicle owners. When revenues stalled, it decided to expand its core to hotel mini-bars. It also began developing additional products for its RV customers—including air-conditioning and water-purification systems. Dometic now commands 75% of the world market share for RV interior systems.

Harness Your Hidden Assets

Hidden assets can spur fresh growth from your new core

defense spending declined sharply. To avoid being stranded by the receding profit pool, it sold off many of its units and redefined the company around just three core businesses where it held substantial advantages: submarines, electronics, and information systems.

The second reason is *inherently inferior economics.* These often come to light when a new competitor enters the field unburdened by structures and costs that an older company cannot readily shake off. General Motors saw this in competition with Toyota, just as Compaq did *if* they provide clear, measurable differentiation from competitors; tangible added value for customers; and a robust profit pool. Hidden assets can be:

- **Undervalued businesses.** General Electric identified an underutilized internal business unit: GE Capital. Fueled by new investment, the division made more than 220 acquisitions over 15 years. Today, GE Capital accounts for 32% of GE's profits.

- **Untapped customer insights.** Harman International, which makes high-end audio equipment, realized people were spending more time in their cars and many drivers were music lovers accustomed to high-end equipment at home. Harman acquired a firm with expertise in designing audio systems for high-end cars. Today, its market value is 40 times greater than in 1993.

- **Underexploited capabilities.** A company's existing capabilities can often be better utilized to spur growth—especially when combined with new capabilities.

Example: Apple capitalized on its strengths in design, brand management, user interface, and easy-to-use software to create the iPod. But it needed to acquire expertise in the music business and digital rights management. Once it had, Apple gained access to content by signing up the top four music companies before rivals did—creating the successful iTunes Music Store.

with Dell. Other well-known examples include Kmart (vis-à-vis Wal-Mart) and Xerox (vis-à-vis Canon). Occasionally a company sees the clouds gathering and is able to respond effectively. The Port of Singapore Authority (now PSA International), for example, fought off threats from Malaysia and other upstart competitors by slashing costs and identifying new ways to add value for customers. But sometimes the economics are driven by laws or entrenched arrangements that a company cannot change.

The third reason to rethink a core strategy is *a growth formula that cannot be sustained*. A manufacturer of a specialized consumer product—cell phones, say—might find its growth stalling as the market reaches saturation or competitors replicate its once unique source of differentiation. Or a retailer like Home Depot might see its growth slow as competitors like Lowe's catch up. A company that has prospered by simply reproducing its business model may run out of new territory to conquer: Think of the difficulties Wal-Mart has encountered as the cost-benefit ratio of further expansion shifts unfavorably. The core business of a mining company might expire as its mines become depleted. In all such circumstances, finding a new formula for growth depends on finding a new core.

For most of the companies my team and I studied, recognition that the core business had faltered came very late. The optical instruments maker PerkinElmer, the diamond merchant De Beers, the audio equipment manufacturer Harman International—these were all companies in deep crisis when they began their redefinition. Is it inevitable that companies will be blindsided in this way? Or can a management team learn to see early signs that its core strategy is losing relevance?

With that possibility in mind, it would seem reasonable to periodically assess the fundamental vitality of your business. The exhibit "Evaluate your core business" offers a tool for doing so. Its first question looks at the core in terms of the customers it serves. How profitable are they—and how loyal? Arriving at the answers can be difficult, but no undertaking is more worthwhile;

Evaluate your core business

Five broad questions can help you determine when it is time to redefine your company's core business. For most companies, the answers to these questions can be found by examining the categories listed next to each one.

If the answers reveal that large shifts are about to take place in two or more of these five areas, your company is heading into turbulence; you need to reexamine the fundamentals of your core strategy and even the core itself.

Question	Take a close look at
1 What is the state of our core customers?	■ profitability ■ market share ■ retention rate ■ measures of customer loyalty and advocacy ■ share of wallet
2 What is the state of our core differentiation?	■ definition and metrics of differentiation ■ relative cost position ■ business models of emerging competitors ■ increasing or decreasing differentiation
3 What is the state of our industry's profit pools?	■ size, growth, and stability ■ share of profit pools captured ■ boundaries ■ shifts and projections ■ high costs and prices
4 What is the state of our core capabilities?	■ inventory of key capabilities ■ relative importance ■ gaps vis-à-vis competitors and vis-à-vis future core needs
5 What is the state of our culture and organization?	■ loyalty and undesired attrition ■ capacity and stress points ■ alignment and agreement with objectives ■ energy and motivation ■ bottlenecks to growth

strategy goes nowhere unless it begins with the customer. The second question probes your company's key sources of differentiation and asks whether they are strengthening or eroding. The third focuses on your industry's profit pools, a perspective that is often neglected in the quest for revenue and market share growth. Where are the best profits to be found? Who earns them now? How might that change? The fourth examines your company's capabilities—a topic we shall soon turn to—and the fifth assesses your organization's culture and readiness to change.

At the least, managers who go through this exercise tend to spot areas of weakness to be shored up. More dramatically, they may save a business from going under. Note, however, that no scoring system is attached to this diagnostic tool—there is no clearly defined point at which a prescription for strategic redefinition is issued. That would lend false precision to what must be a judgment call by a seasoned management team. The value of the exercise is to ensure that the right questions are taken into account and, by being asked consistently over time, highlight changes that may constitute growing threats to a company's core.

Recognizing the Makings of a New Core

Management teams react in different ways when they reach the conclusion that a core business is under severe threat. Some decide to defend the status quo. Others want to transform their companies all at once through a big merger. Some leap into a hot new market.

Such strategies are inordinately risky. (Our analysis suggests that the odds of success are less than one in ten for the first two strategies, and only about one in seven for the third.) The companies we found to be most successful in remaking themselves proceeded in a way that left less to chance. Consider, for example, the transformation of the Swedish company Dometic.

Dometic's roots go back to 1922, when two engineering students named Carl Munters and Baltzar von Platen applied what was known as absorption technology to refrigeration. Whereas most household refrigerators use compressors driven by electric motors to generate cold, their refrigerator had no moving parts and no need for electricity; only a source of heat, as simple as a propane tank, was required. So the absorption refrigerator is particularly useful in places like boats and recreational vehicles, where electric current is hard to come by. In 1925 AB Electrolux acquired the patent rights. The division responsible for absorption refrigerators later became the independent Dometic Group.

By 1973 Dometic was still a small company, with revenues of just 80 million kronor (about U.S. $16.9 million). Worse, it was losing money. Then Sven Stork, an executive charged with fixing the ailing Electrolux product line, began to breathe new life into the business. Stork, who went on to become president and CEO of the company, moved aggressively into the hotel minibar market, where the absorption refrigerator's silent operation had a real advantage over conventional technology. Fueled by those sales, Dometic grew and was able to acquire some of its competitors.

The real breakthrough came when Stork's team focused more closely on the RV market, which was just then beginning to explode. The point wasn't to sell more refrigerators to the RV segment; the company's market share within that segment was already nearly 100%. Rather, it was to add other products to the Dometic line, such as air-conditioning, automated awnings, generators, and systems for cooking, lighting, sanitation, and water purification. As Stork explains, "We decided to make the RV into something that you could really live in. The idea was obvious to people who knew the customers, yet it took a while to convince the manufacturers and especially the rest of our own organization." These moves fundamentally shifted the company's core. Dometic was no longer about absorption refrigeration: It was about RV interior systems and the formidable channel power gained by selling all its products through the same dealers and installers. That channel power allowed Dometic to pull off a move that enhanced its cost structure dramatically. The company streamlined its go-to-market approach in the United States by skipping a distribution layer that had always existed and approaching RV dealers directly. "We prepared for the risks like a military operation," Stork recalls, "and it was a fantastic hit. We were the only company large enough to pull this off. It let us kill off competitors faster than they could come out of the bushes." By 2005 Dometic had grown to KR 7.3 billion, or roughly U.S. $1.2 billion. No longer part of Electrolux (the private equity firm EQT bought it in 2001 and sold it to the investment firm BC Partners a few years later), the company was highly profitable and commanded 75% of the world market share for RV interior systems.

Dometic's story of growth and redefinition is especially instructive because it features all the elements we've seen repeatedly across the successful core-redefining companies we've studied. These are: (1) gradualism during transformation, (2) the discovery and use of hidden assets, (3) underlying leadership economics central to the strategy, and (4) a move from one repeatable formula that is unique to the company to another. "Gradualism" refers to the fact that Dometic never made anything like a "bet the company" move—often tempting when a business is on the ropes, but almost always a loser's game. As in the other cases of strategic renewal we studied, it redefined its core business by shifting its center of gravity along an existing vector of growth. To do this, it relied on hidden assets—resources or capabilities that it had not yet capitalized on. In Dometic's case, the treasure was its understanding of and access to customers in the RV market.

Leadership economics is a hallmark of almost every great strategy; when we see a situation in which the rich get richer, this is the phenomenon at work. Consider that most industries have more than six competitors, but usually more than 75% of the profit pool is captured by the top two. Of those two, the one with the greatest market power typically captures 70% of total profits and 75% of profits above the cost of capital. When Dometic focused on a defined market where it could stake out a leadership position, enormous financial benefits followed.

Its new growth formula offers the same kind of repeatability the old one did. Recall that Dometic's first focus was on applications for absorption refrigeration, which it pursued product by product, one of which was for RVs. The new formula angled off into a sequence of interior components for the RV customer base. Recently, as RV sales have slowed, Dometic has moved into interior systems for "live-in" vehicles in general, including boats and long-haul trucks.

Where Assets Hide

The importance of a company's overlooked, undervalued, or underutilized assets to its strategic regeneration cannot be overstated. In 21 of the 25 companies we examined, a hidden asset was the centerpiece of the new strategy.

Some of their stories are well known. A few years ago, a struggling Apple realized that its flair for software, user-friendly product design, and imaginative marketing could be applied to more than just computers—in particular, to a little device for listening to music. Today Apple's iPod-based music business accounts for nearly 50% of the company's revenues and 40% of profits—a new core. IBM's Global Services Group was once a tiny services and network-operations unit, not even a stand-alone business within IBM. By 2001 it was larger than all of IBM's hardware business and accounted for roughly two-thirds of the company's market value.

Why would well-established companies even have hidden assets? Shouldn't those assets have been put to work or disposed of long since? Actually, large, complex organizations always acquire more skills, capabilities, and business platforms than they can focus on at any one time. Some are necessarily neglected—and once they have been neglected for a while, a company's leaders often continue to ignore them or discount their value. But then something happens: Market conditions change, or perhaps the company acquires new capabilities that complement its forgotten ones. Suddenly the ugly ducklings in the backyard begin to look like swans in training.

The real question, then, is how to open management's eyes to the hidden assets in its midst. One way is to identify the richest hunting grounds. Our research suggests that hidden assets tend to fall into three categories: undervalued business platforms, untapped insights into customers, and underexploited capabilities. The exhibit "Where does your future lie?" details the types of assets we've seen exploited in each category. For a better understanding of how these assets came to light, let's look at some individual examples.

Undervalued Business Platforms

PerkinElmer was once the market leader in optical electronics for analytical instruments, such as spectrophotometers and gas chromatographs. Its optical capabilities were so strong that the company was chosen to manufacture the Hubble Space Telescope's mirrors and sighting equipment for NASA. Yet by 1993 PerkinElmer, its core product lines under attack by lower-cost and more innovative competitors, had stalled out. Revenues were

Where does your future lie?

If the core of your business is nearing depletion, the temptation may be great to venture dramatically away from it—to rely on a major acquisition, for instance, in order to establish a foothold in a new, booming industry. But the history of corporate transformation shows you're more likely to be successful if you seek change in your own backyard.

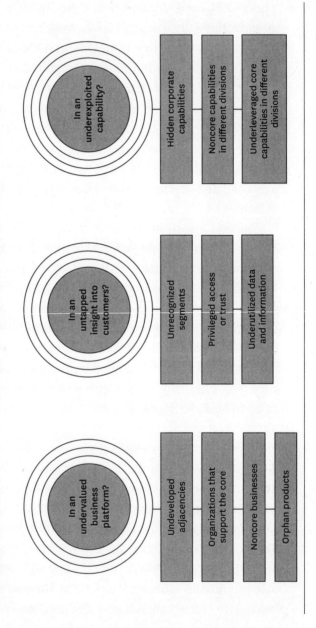

stuck at $1.2 billion, exactly where they had been ten years earlier, and the market value of the company had eroded along with its earnings; the bottom line showed a loss of $83 million in 1993. In 1995 the board hired a new CEO, Tony White, to renew the company's strategy and performance and, if necessary, to completely redefine its core business.

As White examined the range of product lines and the customer segments served, he noticed a hidden asset that could rescue the company. In the early 1990s, PerkinElmer had branched out in another direction—developing products to amplify DNA—through a strategic alliance with Cetus Corporation. In the process, the company obtained rights to cutting-edge procedures known as polymerase chain reaction technology—a key life-sciences platform. In 1993, the company also acquired a small Silicon Valley life-sciences equipment company, Applied Biosystems (AB)—one more line of instruments to be integrated into PerkinElmer's.

White began to conceive of a redefined core built around analytical instruments for the fast-growing segment of life-sciences labs. The AB instruments in the company's catalog, if reorganized and given appropriate resources and direction, could have greater potential than even the original core. White says, "I was struck by how misconceived it was to tear AB apart and distribute its parts across the functions in the organization. I thought, 'Here is a company whose management does not see what they have.' So one of the first steps I took was to begin to reassemble the parts of AB. I appointed a new president of the division and announced that I was going to re-form the core of the company over a three-year period around this unique platform with leadership in key life-sciences detection technology."

Over the next three years, White and his team separated PerkinElmer's original core business and all the life-sciences products and services into two organizations. The employees in the analytical instruments division were given incentives to meet an aggressive cost reduction and cash flow target and told that the division would be spun off as a separate business or sold to a strong partner. Meanwhile, White set up a new data and diagnostics subsidiary, Celera Genomics, which, fueled by the passion of the scientist Craig Venter, famously went on to sequence the complete human genome. Celera and AB were combined into a new core business organization, a holding company christened Applera.

While Celera garnered the headlines, AB became the gold standard in the sequencing instrument business, with the leading market share. Today it has revenues of $1.9 billion and a healthy net income of $275 million. Meanwhile, the original instrument company was sold to the Massachusetts-based EG&G. (Soon after, EG&G changed its corporate name to PerkinElmer—and has since prospered from a combination that redefined its own core.)

The PerkinElmer-to-Applera transformation offers several lessons. The first is that a hidden asset may be a collection of products and customer relationships in different areas of a company that can be collected to form a new core. The second lesson is the power of market leadership: Finding a subcore of leadership buried in the company and building on it in a focused way created something that started smaller than the original combination but became much bigger and stronger. The third lesson lies in the concept of shrinking to grow. Though it sounds paradoxical and is organizationally difficult for companies to come to grips with, this is one of the most underused and underappreciated growth strategies. (See the sidebar "Shrinking to Grow.")

Creating a new core based on a previously over-looked business platform is more common than one might think. General Electric, for instance, like IBM, identified an internal business unit—GE Capital—that was undervalued and underutilized. Fueled by new attention and investment, the once sleepy division made more than 170 acquisitions over a ten-year period, propelling GE's growth. By 2005 GE Capital accounted for 35% of the parent corporation's profits. Nestlé discovered that it had a number of food and drink products designed to be consumed outside the home. Like the original PerkinElmer, it assembled these products into a new unit, Nestlé Food Services; developed a unified strategy; and effectively created the core of a new multibillion-dollar business.

Untapped Insights into Customers

Most large companies gather considerable amounts of data about the people and businesses that buy their wares. But it's not always clear how much they actually know about those customers. In a recent series of business seminars I held for management teams, the participants took an online survey. Though nearly all came

Shrinking to Grow

WHEN A COMPANY UNCOVERS an underutilized source of leadership economics, sometimes the best response is to "double down" on its investment in that area. A bold version of this is actually shrinking to grow. Consider the example of Royal Vopak.

If you are not in the oil or chemicals business, you may not be familiar with Vopak, but it is the world leader in independent tank storage of bulk oil and chemicals, operating in 75 port locations from Rotterdam to Houston to Singapore. Vopak traces its roots back to a time when the Netherlands was the wealthiest and most powerful country in the world, owing to its role as a center for shipping and trade with the Far East. The origins of Vopak lie in a company that was founded in 1616, by a group of porters on the docks of Amsterdam, for the purpose of loading and unloading ship cargoes.

By 2000 Vopak was enjoying sales of €5.6 billion, with positions in shipping, chemical distribution, and port storage facilities. Its storage business was the most profitable. When Vopak's profits suffered and its stock price came under severe pressure, plummeting from €25 per share in June 1999 to €12 in July 2002, the company took decisive action. It spun off everything but the

from well-regarded companies, fewer than 25% agreed with the simple statement "We understand our customers." In a 2004 Bain survey, we asked respondents to identify the most important capabilities their companies could acquire to trigger a new wave of growth. "Capabilities to understand our core customers more deeply" topped the list.

For just this reason, insights into and relationships with customers are often hidden assets. A company may discover that one neglected customer segment storage business, reducing the sales volume of the company to €750 million. But Vopak did not stop there: It even sold some of its storage portfolio, further reducing its size.

What was the result? Amazingly, the company's market value increased beyond its original level, as the stock price rebounded to €30 in May 2006. Furthermore, the stronger, well-funded business began to grow again—both organically and through acquisitions and new port locations. During the first half of 2006, Vopak's revenues grew by 17% and its earnings by 28%, in an inherently low-growth industry. John Paul Broeders, the chairman of the executive board, says, "Without shrinking first, we would never have created the resources, the management focus, and a stable platform to begin to grow again as we have."

Shrink-to-grow strategies are not an end in themselves, but they can pave the way for redefinition. These moves have a very high success rate when it comes to increasing a company's value and liberating one of the cores to strengthen and grow, provided it's given additional resources. Indeed, another three of our 25 case studies in successful core redefinition relied on this tactic: PerkinElmer, Samsung, and GUS.

holds the key to unprecedented growth. It may find that it is in a position of influence over its customers, perhaps because of the trust and reputation it enjoys, and that it has not fully developed this position. Or it may find that it has proprietary data that can be used to alter, deepen, or broaden its customer relationships. All these can stimulate growth around a new core.

Harman International, a maker of high-end audio equipment, redefined its core around an unexploited customer segment. In the early 1990s it was focused primarily on the consumer and professional audio markets, with less than 10% of revenues coming from the original-equipment automotive market. But its growth had stagnated and its profits were near zero. In 1993 Sidney Harman, a cofounder, who had left the company to serve as U.S. deputy secretary of commerce, returned as CEO in an attempt to rejuvenate the company.

Harman cast a curious eye on the automotive segment. He realized that people were spending more time in their cars, and that many drivers were music lovers accustomed to high-end equipment at home. Hoping to beef up the company's sales in this sector, he acquired the German company Becker, which supplied radios to Mercedes-Benz. One day when Harman was visiting their plant, some Becker engineers demonstrated how new digital hardware allowed the company to create high-performance audio equipment in a much smaller space than before. That, Harman says, was the turning point. He invested heavily in digital to create branded high-end automotive "infotainment" systems. The systems proved to have immense appeal both for car buyers and for car manufacturers, who enjoyed healthy margins on the equipment. Based largely on its success in the automotive market, Harman's market value increased 40-fold from 1993 to 2005.

It is somewhat unusual, of course, to find an untapped customer segment that is poised for such rapid growth. But it isn't at all unusual for a company to discover that its relationships with customers are deeper than it realized, or that it has more knowledge about customers than it has put to work. Hyperion Solutions,

---

Seven steps to a new core business

1 Define the core of your business. Reach consensus on the true state of the core.

2 Assess the core's full potential and the durability of its key differentiation.

3 Develop a point of view about the future, and define the status quo.

4 Identify the full range of options for redefining the core from the inside and from the outside.

5 Identify your hidden assets, and ask whether they create new options or enable others.

6 Use key criteria (leadership, profit pool, repeatability, chances of implementation) in deciding which assets to employ in redefining your core.

7 Set up a program office to help initiate, track, and manage course corrections.

---

a producer of financial software, was able to reinvent itself around new products and a new sales-and-service platform precisely because corporate finance departments had come to depend on its software for financial consolidation and SEC reporting. "We totally underestimated how much they relied upon us for this very technical and sensitive part of their job," says Jeff Rodek, formerly Hyperion's CEO and now the executive chairman. American Express transformed its credit-card business on the basis of previously unutilized knowledge of how different customer segments used the cards and what other products might appeal to them. Even De Beers, long known for its monopolistic practices in the diamond industry, recently redefined its core around consumer and customer relationships. De Beers, of course, had long-standing relationships with everyone in the industry. When its competitive landscape changed with the emergence of new rivals, De Beers leaders Nicky Oppenheimer and Gary Ralfe decided to make the company's strong brand and its unique image and relationships the basis of a major strategic redefinition. The company liquidated 80% of its inventory—the stockpile that had allowed it for so long to stabilize diamond prices—and created a new business model. It built up its brand through advertising. It developed new product ideas for its distributors and jewelers, and sponsored ad campaigns to market them to consumers. As a result, the estimated value of De Beers's diamond business increased nearly tenfold. The company is still in the business of selling rough diamonds, but its core is no longer about controlling supply—it's about serving consumers and customers.

Underexploited Capabilities
Hidden business platforms and hidden customer insights are assets that companies already possess; in theory, all that remains is for management to uncover them and put them to work. Capabilities—the ability to perform specific tasks over and over again—are different. Any capability is potentially available to any company. What matters is how individual companies combine multiple capabilities into "activity systems," as Michael Porter calls them, meaning combinations of business processes that create hard-to-replicate competitive advantage. IKEA's successful business formula, Porter

argued in his 1996 HBR article "What Is Strategy?," can be traced to a strong and unique set of linked capabilities, including global sourcing, design for assembly, logistics, and cost management.

An underexploited capability, therefore, can be an engine of growth if and only if it can combine with a company's other capabilities to produce something distinctly new and better. Consider the Danish company Novozymes, now a world leader in the development and production of high-quality enzymes. When it was spun off from its parent corporation in 2000, Novozymes was still largely dependent on relatively low-tech commodity enzymes such as those used in detergents.

Steen Riisgaard, the company's chief executive, set out to change that, and the key was Novozymes's underutilized scientific capability. Riisgaard focused the company's R&D on the creation of bioengineered specialty enzymes. Its scientists worked closely with customers in order to design the enzymes precisely to their specifications. If a customer wanted to remove grease stains from laundry at unusually low temperatures, for instance, Novozymes would collect possible enzyme-producing microorganisms from all over the world, determine which one produced the enzyme closest to what was needed, remove the relevant gene, and insert the gene into an organism that could safely be produced at high volume. Riisgaard likens the process to finding a needle in a haystack, except that Novozymes uses state-of-the-art technology to single out the haystacks and accelerate the search. Such capabilities have shortened product development from five years to two and have set Novozymes apart from its competitors.

Of course, a company may find that it needs to acquire new capabilities to complement those it already has before it can create a potent activity system. Apple indisputably capitalized on its strengths in design, brand management, user interface, and elegant, easy-to-use software in creating the iPod. But it also needed expertise in the music business and in digital rights management. Once it had those, Apple gained access to content by signing up the top four recording companies before competitors could and developing the iTunes Music Store. It also created a brilliantly functional approach to digital rights management with its Fairplay software, which ensures that the music companies obtain a highly controllable revenue stream. This combination of existing and new capabilities proved transformational for Apple.

The highest form of capability development is to create a unique set of capabilities—no longer hidden—that can build one growth platform after another, repeatedly giving a company competitive advantage in multiple markets. Though difficult, this is a strong temptation; indeed, it has proved to be a siren song for many. But a few companies, such as Emerson Electric, Valspar, Medtronic, and Johnson & Johnson, have managed to avoid the rocks. A lesser-known example is Danaher, which only 20 years ago was a midsize company with $617 million in revenues and almost all its business concentrated in industrial tool markets. Danaher developed a set of procedures whereby it can identify acquisitions and then add value to the acquired companies through the so-called Danaher Business System. The system has several phases and dimensions, including cultural values, productivity improvement, sourcing techniques, and a distinctive approach to measurement and control. It has allowed Danaher to expand into six strategic platforms and 102 subunits spanning a wide range of industrial applications, from electronic testing to environmental services. The company's stock price has risen by more than 5,000% since 1987, outpacing the broader market by a factor of more than five.

It's somewhat maddening how the assets explored here—PerkinElmer's undervalued business platform, Harman's untapped customer insights, Novozymes's underexploited capabilities—can be so obvious in hindsight and yet were so hard to appreciate at the time. Will you be any better able to see what is under your nose? One thing seems clear: Your next core business will not announce itself with fanfare. More likely, you will arrive at it by a painstaking audit of the areas outlined in this article.

The first step is simply to shine a light on the dark corners of your business and identify assets that are candidates for a new core. Once identified, these assets must be assessed. Do they offer the potential of clear, measurable differentiation from your competition? Can they provide tangible added value for your customers? Is there a robust profit pool that they can help you target? Can you acquire the additional capabilities you may need to implement the redefinition? Like the four

essentials of a good golf swing, each of these requirements sounds easily met; the difficulty comes in meeting all four at once. Apple's iPod-based redefinition
succeeded precisely because the company could answer every question in the affirmative. A negative
answer to any one of them would have torpedoed the
entire effort.

A Growing Imperative for Management

Learning to perform such assessments and to take
gradual, confident steps toward a new core business is
increasingly central to the conduct of corporate management. Look, for example, at the fate of the *Fortune*
500 companies in 1994. A research team at Bain found
that a decade later 153 of those companies had either
gone bankrupt or been acquired, and another 130 had
engineered a fundamental shift in their core business
strategy. In other words, nearly six out of ten faced serious threats to their survival or independence during the
decade, and only about half of this group were able to
meet the threat successfully by redefining their core
business.

Why do so many companies face the need to transform themselves? Think of the cycle that long-lived companies commonly go through: They prosper first by
focusing relentlessly on what they do well, next by
expanding on that core to grow, and then, when the core
has lost its relevance, by redefining themselves and
focusing anew on a different core strength. It seems clear
that this focus-expand-redefine cycle has accelerated

over the decades. Companies move from one phase to another faster than they once did. The forces behind the acceleration are for the most part well known. New technologies lower costs and shorten product life cycles. New competitors—currently in China and India—shake up whole industries. Capital, innovation, and management talent flow more freely and more quickly around the globe. The churn caused by all this is wide-ranging. The average holding period for a share of common stock has declined from three years in the 1980s to nine months today. The average life span of companies has dropped from 14 years to just over ten, and the average tenure of CEOs has declined from eight years a decade ago to less than five today.

Business leaders are acutely aware of these waves of change and their ramifications. In 2004 my colleagues and I surveyed 259 senior executives around the world about the challenges they faced. More than 80% of them indicated that the productive lives of their strategies were getting shorter. Seventy-two percent believed that their leading competitor would be a different company in five years. Sixty-five percent believed that they would need to restructure the business model that served their primary customers. As the focus-expand-redefine cycle continues to pick up speed, each year will find more companies in that fateful third phase, where redefinition is essential. For most, the right way forward will lie in assets that are hidden from view—in neglected businesses, unused customer insights, and latent capabilities that, once harnessed, can propel new growth.

CHRIS ZOOK leads the Global Strategy Practice at Bain & Company and is the author of *Unstoppable* (Harvard Business Review Press, 2007), from which this article is adapted.

Originally published in April 2007.   Reprint R0704D

Disruptive Technologies

Catching the Wave
by Joseph L. Bower and Clayton M. Christensen

ONE OF THE MOST CONSISTENT PATTERNS in business is the failure of leading companies to stay at the top of their industries when technologies or markets change. Goodyear and Firestone entered the radial-tire market quite late. Xerox let Canon create the small-copier market. Bucyrus-Erie allowed Caterpillar and Deere to take over the mechanical excavator market. Sears gave way to Wal-Mart.

The pattern of failure has been especially striking in the computer industry. IBM dominated the mainframe market but missed by years the emergence of mini-computers, which were technologically much simpler than mainframes. Digital Equipment dominated the minicomputer market with innovations like its VAX architecture but missed the personal-computer market almost completely. Apple Computer led the world of personal computing and established the standard for user-friendly computing but lagged five years behind the leaders in bringing its portable computer to market.

Why is it that companies like these invest aggressively—and successfully—in the technologies necessary to retain their current customers but then fail to make certain other technological investments that customers of the future will demand? Undoubtedly, bureaucracy, arrogance, tired executive blood, poor planning, and short-term investment horizons have all played a role. But a more fundamental reason lies at the heart of the paradox: leading companies succumb to one of the most popular, and valuable, management dogmas. They stay close to their customers.

Although most managers like to think they are in control, customers wield extraordinary power in directing a company's investments. Before managers decide to launch a technology, develop a product, build a plant, or establish new channels of distribution, they must look to their customers first: Do their customers want it? How big will the market be? Will the investment be profitable? The more astutely managers ask and answer these questions, the more completely their investments will be aligned with the needs of their customers.

This is the way a well-managed company should operate. Right? But what happens when customers reject a new technology, product concept, or way of doing business because it does *not* address their needs as effectively as a company's current approach? The large photocopying centers that represented the core of Xerox's customer base at first had no use for small, slow tabletop copiers. The excavation contractors that had

Idea in Brief

Goodyear, Xerox, Bucyrus-Erie, Digital. Leading companies all—yet they all failed to stay at the top of their industries when technologies or markets changed radically. That's disturbing enough, but the reason for the failure is downright alarming. The very processes that successful, well-managed companies use to serve the rapidly growing needs of their current customers can leave them highly vulnerable when market-changing technologies appear.

When a technology that has the potential for revolutionizing an industry emerges, established companies typically see it as unattractive: it's not something their mainstream customers want, and its projected profit margins aren't sufficient to cover big-company cost structures. As a result, the new technology tends to get ignored in favor of what's currently popular with the best customers. But then another company steps in to bring the innovation to a new market. Once the disruptive technology becomes established there, smaller-scale innovations rapidly raise the technology's performance on attributes that *mainstream* customers value.

What happens next is akin to the rapid, final moves leading to checkmate. The new technology invades the established market. By the time the established supplier—with its high overhead and profit margin requirements—wakes up and smells the coffee, its competitive disadvantage is insurmountable.

relied on Bucyrus-Erie's big-bucket steam- and diesel-powered cable shovels didn't want hydraulic excavators because initially they were small and weak. IBM's large commercial, government, and industrial customers saw no immediate use for minicomputers. In each instance, companies listened to their customers, gave them the product performance they were looking for, and, in the end, were hurt by the very technologies their customers led them to ignore.

Idea in Practice

At issue here is a key distinction:

- **Sustaining innovation** maintains a steady rate of product improvement.

- **Disruptive innovation** often sacrifices performance along dimensions that are important to current customers and offers a very different package of attributes that are not (yet) valued by those customers. At the same time, the new attributes can open up entirely new markets. For example, Sony's early transistor radios sacrificed sound fidelity, but they created a new market for small, portable radios.

Staying focused on your main customers can work so well that you overlook disruptive technologies. The consequences can be far more disastrous than a missed opportunity. Case in point: not one of the independent hard-disk drive companies that existed in 1976 is still around today.

To prevent disruptive technologies from slipping through their fingers, established organizations must learn how to identify and nurture innovations on a more modest scale—so that small orders are meaningful, ill-defined markets have time to mature, and overhead is low enough to permit early

We have seen this pattern repeatedly in an ongoing study of leading companies in a variety of industries that have confronted technological change. The research shows that most well-managed, established companies are consistently ahead of their industries in developing and commercializing new technologies—from incremental improvements to radically new approaches—as long as those technologies address the next-generation performance needs of their customers. However, these same companies are rarely in the forefront of commercializing new technologies that don't initially meet the profits. Here's a four-step guide:

1. **Determine whether the technology is disruptive or sustaining.** Ask the technical folks—they're more attuned than marketing and financial managers to which technologies have the potential to revolutionize the market.

2. **Define the strategic significance of the disruptive technology.** Your best customers are the last people to ask about this— sustaining technologies are what they care about.

3. **Locate the initial market for the disruptive technology.** If the market doesn't yet exist, conventional market research won't give you the information you need. So create it instead, by experimenting rapidly, iteratively, and inexpensively—with both the product and the market.

4. **House the disruptive technology in an independent entity.** For a disruptive technology to thrive, it can't be required to compete with established products for company resources.

needs of mainstream customers and appeal only to small or emerging markets.

Using the rational, analytical investment processes that most well-managed companies have developed, it is nearly impossible to build a cogent case for diverting resources from known customer needs in established markets to markets and customers that seem insignificant or do not yet exist. After all, meeting the needs of established customers and fending off competitors takes all the resources a company has, and then some. In well-managed companies, the processes used to identify customers' needs, forecast technological trends, assess profitability, allocate resources across competing proposals for investment, and take new products to market are focused—for all the right reasons—on current customers and markets. These processes are designed to weed out proposed products and technologies that do *not* address customers' needs.

In fact, the processes and incentives that companies use to keep focused on their main customers work so well that they blind those companies to important new technologies in emerging markets. Many companies have learned the hard way the perils of ignoring new technologies that do not initially meet the needs of mainstream customers. For example, although personal computers did not meet the requirements of mainstream minicomputer users in the early 1980s, the computing power of the desktop machines improved at a much faster rate than minicomputer users' *demands* for computing power did. As a result, personal computers caught up with the computing needs of many of the customers of Wang, Prime, Nixdorf, Data General, and Digital Equipment. Today they are performance-competitive with minicomputers in many applications. For the minicomputer makers, keeping close to mainstream customers and ignoring what were initially low-performance desktop technologies used by seemingly insignificant customers in emerging markets was a rational decision—but one that proved disastrous.

The technological changes that damage established companies are usually not radically new or difficult from a *technological* point of view. They do, however, have two important characteristics: First, they typically present a different package of performance attributes— ones that, at least at the outset, are not valued by existing customers. Second, the performance attributes that existing customers do value improve at such a rapid rate that the new technology can later invade those established markets. Only at this point will mainstream customers want the technology. Unfortunately for the established suppliers, by then it is often too late: the pioneers of the new technology dominate the market.

It follows, then, that senior executives must first be able to spot the technologies that seem to fall into this category. Next, to commercialize and develop the new technologies, managers must protect them from the processes and incentives that are geared to serving established customers. And the only way to protect them is to create organizations that are completely independent from the mainstream business.

No industry demonstrates the danger of staying too close to customers more dramatically than the hard-disk-drive industry. Between 1976 and 1992, disk-drive performance improved at a stunning rate: the physical size of a 100-megabyte (MB) system shrank from 5,400 to 8 cubic inches, and the cost per MB fell from $560 to $5. Technological change, of course, drove these breathtaking achievements. About half of the improvement came from a host of radical advances that were critical to continued improvements in disk-drive performance; the other half came from incremental advances.

The pattern in the disk-drive industry has been repeated in many other industries: the leading, established companies have consistently led the industry in developing and adopting new technologies that their customers demanded—even when those technologies required completely different technological competencies and manufacturing capabilities from the ones the companies had. In spite of this aggressive technological posture, no single disk-drive manufacturer has been able to dominate the industry for more than a few years. A series of companies have entered the business and risen to prominence, only to be toppled by newcomers who pursued technologies that at first did not meet the needs of mainstream customers. As a result, not one of the independent disk-drive companies that existed in 1976 survives today.

To explain the differences in the impact of certain kinds of technological innovations on a given industry, the concept of *performance trajectories*—the rate at which the performance of a product has improved, and is expected to improve, over time—can be helpful. Almost every industry has a critical performance trajectory. In mechanical excavators, the critical trajectory is the annual improvement in cubic yards of earth moved per minute. In photocopiers, an important performance trajectory is improvement in number of copies per minute. In disk drives, one crucial measure of performance is storage capacity, which has advanced 50% each year on average for a given size of drive.

Different types of technological innovations affect performance trajectories in different ways. On the one hand, *sustaining* technologies tend to maintain a rate of improvement; that is, they give customers something more or better in the attributes they already value. For example, thin-film components in disk drives, which replaced conventional ferrite heads and oxide disks between 1982 and 1990, enabled information to be recorded more densely on disks. Engineers had been pushing the limits of the performance they could wring from ferrite heads and oxide disks, but the drives employing these technologies seemed to have reached the natural limits of an *S* curve. At that point, new thin-film technologies emerged that restored—or sustained—the historical trajectory of performance improvement.

On the other hand, *disruptive* technologies introduce a very different package of attributes from the one mainstream customers historically value, and they often perform far worse along one or two dimensions that are particularly important to those customers. As a rule, mainstream customers are unwilling to use a disruptive product in applications they know and understand. At first, then, disruptive technologies tend to be used and valued only in new markets or new applications; in fact, they generally make possible the emergence of new markets. For example, Sony's early transistor radios sacrificed sound fidelity but created a market for portable radios by offering a new and different package of attributes—small size, light weight, and portability.

In the history of the hard-disk-drive industry, the leaders stumbled at each point of disruptive technological change: when the diameter of disk drives shrank from the original 14 inches to 8 inches, then to 5.25 inches, and finally to 3.5 inches. Each of these new architectures initially offered the market substantially less storage capacity than the typical user in the established market required. For example, the 8-inch drive offered 20 MB when it was introduced, while the primary market for disk drives at that time—mainframes—required 200 MB on average. Not surprisingly, the leading computer manufacturers rejected the 8-inch architecture at first. As a result, their suppliers, whose mainstream products consisted of 14-inch drives with more than 200 MB of capacity, did not pursue the disruptive products aggressively. The pattern was repeated when the 5.25-inch and 3.5-inch drives emerged: established computer makers rejected the drives as inadequate, and, in turn, their disk-drive suppliers ignored them as well.

But while they offered less storage capacity, the disruptive architectures created other important attributes—internal power supplies and smaller size (8-inch drives); still smaller size and low-cost stepper motors (5.25-inch drives); and ruggedness, light weight, and low-power consumption (3.5-inch drives). From the late 1970s to the mid-1980s, the availability of the three drives made possible the development of new markets for minicomputers, desktop PCs, and portable computers, respectively.

Although the smaller drives represented disruptive technological change, each was technologically straightforward. In fact, there were engineers at many leading companies who championed the new technologies and built working prototypes with bootlegged resources before management gave a formal go-ahead. Still, the leading companies could not move the products through their organizations and into the market in a timely way. Each time a disruptive technology emerged, between one-half and two-thirds of the established manufacturers failed to introduce models employing the new architecture—in stark contrast to their timely launches of critical sustaining technologies. Those companies that finally did launch new models typically lagged behind entrant companies by two years—eons in an industry whose products' life cycles are often two years. Three waves of entrant companies led these revolutions; they first captured the new markets and then dethroned the leading companies in the mainstream markets.

How could technologies that were initially inferior and useful only to new markets eventually threaten leading companies in established markets? Once the disruptive architectures became established in their new markets, sustaining innovations raised each architecture's performance along steep trajectories—so steep that the performance available from each architecture soon satisfied the needs of customers in the established markets. For example, the 5.25-inch drive, whose initial 5 MB of capacity in 1980 was only a fraction of the capacity that the minicomputer market needed, became fully performance-competitive in the minicomputer market by 1986 and in the mainframe market by 1991. (See the graph "How disk-drive performance met market needs.")

A company's revenue and cost structures play a critical role in the way it evaluates proposed technological innovations. Generally, disruptive technologies look financially unattractive to established companies. The

How disk-drive performance met market needs

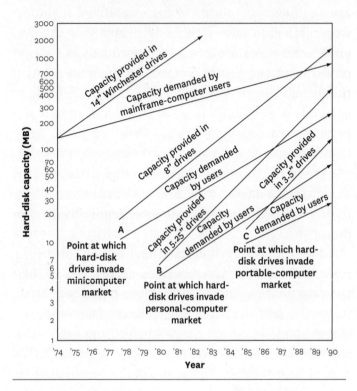

potential revenues from the discernible markets are small, and it is often difficult to project how big the markets for the technology will be over the long term. As a result, managers typically conclude that the technology cannot make a meaningful contribution to corporate growth and, therefore, that it is not worth the management effort required to develop it. In addition, established companies have often installed higher cost structures to serve sustaining technologies than those required by disruptive technologies. As a result, managers typically see themselves as having two choices when deciding whether to pursue disruptive technologies. One is to go *downmarket* and accept the lower profit margins of the emerging markets that the disruptive technologies will initially serve. The other is to go *upmarket* with sustaining technologies and enter market segments whose profit margins are alluringly high. (For example, the margins of IBM's mainframes are still higher than those of PCs). Any rational resource-allocation process in companies serving established markets will choose going upmarket rather than going down.

Managers of companies that have championed disruptive technologies in emerging markets look at the world quite differently. Without the high cost structures of their established counterparts, these companies find the emerging markets appealing. Once the companies have secured a foothold in the markets and improved the performance of their technologies, the established markets above them, served by high-cost suppliers, look appetizing. When they do attack, the entrant companies find the established players to be easy and unprepared opponents because the opponents have been looking upmarket themselves, discounting the threat from below.

It is tempting to stop at this point and conclude that a valuable lesson has been learned: managers can avoid missing the next wave by paying careful attention to potentially disruptive technologies that do *not* meet current customers' needs. But recognizing the pattern and figuring out how to break it are two different things. Although entrants invaded established markets with new technologies three times in succession, none of the established leaders in the disk-drive industry seemed to learn from the experiences of those that fell before them. Management myopia or lack of foresight cannot explain these failures. The problem is that managers keep doing what has worked in the past: serving the rapidly growing needs of their current customers. The processes that successful, well-managed companies have developed to allocate resources among proposed investments are *incapable* of funneling resources into programs that current customers explicitly don't want and whose profit margins seem unattractive.

Managing the development of new technology is tightly linked to a company's investment processes. Most strategic proposals—to add capacity or to develop new products or processes—take shape at the lower levels of organizations in engineering groups or project teams. Companies then use analytical planning and budgeting systems to select from among the candidates competing for funds. Proposals to create new businesses in emerging markets are particularly challenging to assess because they depend on notoriously unreliable estimates of market size. Because managers are evaluated on their ability to place the right bets, it is not surprising that in well-managed companies, mid- and top-level managers back projects in which the market seems assured. By staying close to lead customers, as they have been trained to do, managers focus resources on fulfilling the requirements of those reliable customers that can be served profitably. Risk is reduced—and careers are safeguarded—by giving known customers what they want.

Seagate Technology's experience illustrates the consequences of relying on such resource-allocation processes to evaluate disruptive technologies. By almost-any measure, Seagate, based in Scotts Valley, California, was one of the most successful and aggressively man-aged companies in the history of the microelectronics industry: from its inception in 1980, Seagate's revenues had grown to more than $700 million by 1986. It had pioneered 5.25-inch hard-disk drives and was the main supplier of them to IBM and IBM-compatible personal-computer manufacturers. The company was the lead-ing manufacturer of 5.25-inch drives at the time the disruptive 3.5-inch drives emerged in the mid-1980s.

Engineers at Seagate were the second in the industry to develop working prototypes of 3.5-inch drives. By early 1985, they had made more than 80 such models with a low level of company funding. The engineers for-warded the new models to key marketing executives, and the trade press reported that Seagate was actively developing 3.5-inch drives. But Seagate's principal customers—IBM and other manufacturers of AT-class personal computers—showed no interest in the new drives. They wanted to incorporate 40-MB and 60-MB drives in their next-generation models, and Seagate's early 3.5-inch prototypes packed only 10 MB. In response, Seagate's marketing executives lowered their sales forecasts for the new disk drives.

Manufacturing and financial executives at the company pointed out another drawback to the 3.5-inch drives. According to their analysis, the new drives would never be competitive with the 5.25-inch architecture on a cost-per-megabyte basis—an important metric that Seagate's customers used to evaluate disk drives. Given Seagate's cost structure, margins on the higher-capacity 5.25-inch models therefore promised to be much higher than those on the smaller products.

Senior managers quite rationally decided that the 3.5-inch drive would not provide the sales volume and profit margins that Seagate needed from a new product. A former Seagate marketing executive recalled, "We needed a new model that could become the next ST412 [a 5.25-inch drive generating more than $300 million in annual sales, which was nearing the end of its life cycle]. At the time, the entire market for 3.5-inch drives was less than $50 million. The 3.5-inch drive just didn't fit the bill—for sales or profits."

The shelving of the 3.5-inch drive was *not* a signal that Seagate was complacent about innovation. Seagate subsequently introduced new models of 5.25-inch drives at an accelerated rate and, in so doing, introduced an impressive array of sustaining technological improvements, even though introducing them rendered a significant portion of its manufacturing capacity obsolete.

While Seagate's attention was glued to the personal-computer market, former employees of Seagate and other 5.25-inch drive makers, who had become frustrated by their employers' delays in launching 3.5-inch drives, founded a new company, Conner Peripherals. Conner focused on selling its 3.5-inch drives to companies in emerging markets for portable computers and small-footprint desktop products (PCs that take up a smaller amount of space on a desk). Conner's primary customer was Compaq Computer, a customer that Seagate had never served. Seagate's own prosperity, coupled with Conner's focus on customers who valued different disk-drive attributes (ruggedness, physical volume, and weight), minimized the threat Seagate saw in Conner and its 3.5-inch drives.

From its beachhead in the emerging market for portable computers, however, Conner improved the storage capacity of its drives by 50% per year. By the end of 1987, 3.5-inch drives packed the capacity demanded in the mainstream personal-computer market. At this point, Seagate executives took their company's 3.5-inch drive off the shelf, introducing it to the market as a *defensive* response to the attack of entrant companies like Conner and Quantum Corporation, the other pioneer of 3.5-inch drives. But it was too late.

By then, Seagate faced strong competition. For a while, the company was able to defend its existing market by selling 3.5-inch drives to its established customer base—manufacturers and resellers of full-size personal computers. In fact, a large proportion of its 3.5-inch products continued to be shipped in frames that enabled its customers to mount the drives in computers designed to accommodate 5.25-inch drives. But, in the end, Seagate could only struggle to become a second-tier supplier in the new portable-computer market.

In contrast, Conner and Quantum built a dominant position in the new portable-computer market and then used their scale and experience base in designing and manufacturing 3.5-inch products to drive Seagate from the personal-computer market. In their 1994 fiscal years, the combined revenues of Conner and Quantum exceeded $5 billion.

Seagate's poor timing typifies the responses of many established companies to the emergence of disruptive technologies. Seagate was willing to enter the market for 3.5-inch drives only when it had become large enough to satisfy the company's financial requirements—that is, only when existing customers wanted the new technology. Seagate has survived through its savvy acquisition of Control Data Corporation's disk-drive business in 1990. With CDC's technology base and Seagate's volume-manufacturing expertise, the company has become a powerful player in the business of supplying large-capacity drives for high-end computers. Nonetheless, Seagate has been reduced to a shadow of its former self in the personal-computer market.

It should come as no surprise that few companies, when confronted with disruptive technologies, have been able to overcome the handicaps of size or success. But it can be done. There is a method to spotting and cultivating disruptive technologies.

Determine Whether the Technology is Disruptive or Sustaining

The first step is to decide which of the myriad technologies on the horizon are disruptive and, of those, which are real threats. Most companies have well-conceived processes for identifying and tracking the progress of potentially sustaining technologies, because they are important to serving and protecting current customers. But few have systematic processes in place to identify and track potentially disruptive technologies.

One approach to identifying disruptive technologies is to examine internal disagreements over the development of new products or technologies. Who supports the project and who doesn't? Marketing and financial managers, because of their managerial and financial incentives, will rarely support a disruptive technology. On the other hand, technical personnel with outstanding track records will often persist in arguing that a new market for the technology will emerge—even in the face of opposition from key customers and marketing and financial staff. Disagreement between the two groups often signals a disruptive technology that top-level managers should explore.

Define the Strategic Significance of the Disruptive Technology

The next step is to ask the right people the right questions about the strategic importance of the disruptive technology. Disruptive technologies tend to stall early in strategic reviews because managers either ask the wrong questions or ask the wrong people the right questions. For example, established companies have regular procedures for asking mainstream customers—especially the important accounts where new ideas are actually tested—to assess the value of innovative products.

Generally, these customers are selected because they are the ones striving the hardest to stay ahead of *their* competitors in pushing the performance of *their* products. Hence these customers are most likely to demand the highest performance from their suppliers. For this reason, lead customers are reliably accurate when it comes to assessing the potential of sustaining technologies, but they are reliably *in*accurate when it comes to assessing the potential of disruptive technologies. They are the wrong people to ask.

A simple graph plotting product performance as it is defined in mainstream markets on the vertical axis and time on the horizontal axis can help managers identify both the right questions and the right people to ask. First, draw a line depicting the level of performance and the trajectory of performance improvement that customers have historically enjoyed and are likely to expect in the future. Then locate the estimated initial performance level of the new technology. If the technology is disruptive, the point will lie far below the performance demanded by current customers. (See the graph "How to assess disruptive technologies.")

What is the likely slope of performance improvement of the disruptive technology compared with the slope of performance improvement demanded by existing markets? If knowledgeable technologists believe the new technology might progress faster than the market's demand for performance improvement, then that technology, which does not meet customers' needs today, may very well address them tomorrow. The new technology, therefore, is strategically critical.

How to assess disruptive technologies

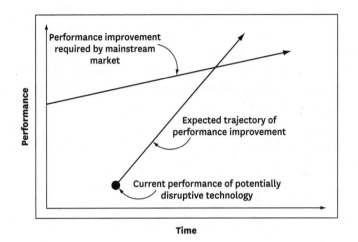

Instead of taking this approach, most managers ask the wrong questions. They compare the anticipated rate of performance improvement of the new technology with that of the established technology. If the new technology has the potential to surpass the established one, the reasoning goes, they should get busy developing it.

Pretty simple. But this sort of comparison, while valid for sustaining technologies, misses the central strategic issue in assessing potentially disruptive technologies. Many of the disruptive technologies we studied *never* surpassed the capability of the old technology. It is the trajectory of the disruptive technology compared with that of the *market* that is significant. For example, the reason the mainframe-computer market is shrinking is not that personal computers outperform mainframes but because personal computers networked with a file server meet the computing and data-storage needs of many organizations effectively. Mainframe-computer makers are reeling not because the performance of personal-computing technology surpassed the performance of mainframe *technology* but because it intersected with the performance demanded by the established *market*.

Consider the graph again. If technologists believe that the new technology will progress at the same rate as the market's demand for performance improvement, the disruptive technology may be slower to invade established markets. Recall that Seagate had targeted personal computing, where demand for hard-disk capacity per computer was growing at 30% per year. Because the capacity of 3.5-inch drives improved at a much faster rate, leading 3.5-inch-drive makers were able to force Seagate out of the market. However, two other 5.25-inch-drive makers, Maxtor and Micropolis, had targeted the engineering-workstation market, in which demand for hard-disk capacity was insatiable. In that market, the trajectory of capacity demanded was essentially parallel to the trajectory of capacity improvement that technologists could supply in the 3.5-inch architecture. As a result, entering the 3.5-inch-drive business was strategically less critical for those companies than it was for Seagate.

Locate the Initial Market for the Disruptive Technology
Once managers have determined that a new technology is disruptive and strategically critical, the next step is to locate the initial markets for that technology. Market

research, the tool that managers have traditionally relied on, is seldom helpful: at the point a company needs to make a strategic commitment to a disruptive technology, no concrete market exists. When Edwin Land asked Polaroid's market researchers to assess the potential sales of his new camera, they concluded that Polaroid would sell a mere 100,000 cameras over the product's lifetime; few people they interviewed could imagine the uses of instant photography.

Because disruptive technologies frequently signal the emergence of new markets or market segments, managers must *create* information about such markets—who the customers will be, which dimensions of product performance will matter most to which customers, what the right price points will be. Managers can create this kind of information only by experimenting rapidly, iteratively, and inexpensively with both the product and the market.

For established companies to undertake such experiments is very difficult. The resource-allocation processes that are critical to profitability and competitiveness will not—and should not—direct resources to markets in which sales will be relatively small. How, then, can an established company probe a market for a disruptive technology? Let start-ups—either ones the company funds or others with no connection to the company—conduct the experiments. Small, hungry organizations are good at placing economical bets, rolling with the punches, and agilely changing product and market strategies in response to feedback from initial forays into the market.

Consider Apple Computer in its start-up days. The company's original product, the Apple I, was a flop when it was launched in 1977. But Apple had not placed a huge bet on the product and had gotten at least *something* into the hands of early users quickly. The company learned a lot from the Apple I about the new technology and about what customers wanted and did not want. Just as important, a group of *customers* learned about what they did and did not want from personal computers. Armed with this information, Apple launched the Apple II quite successfully.

Many companies could have learned the same valuable lessons by watching Apple closely. In fact, some companies pursue an explicit strategy of being *second to invent*—allowing small pioneers to lead the way into uncharted market territory. For instance, IBM let Apple, Commodore, and Tandy define the personal computer. It then aggressively entered the market and built a considerable personal-computer business.

But IBM's relative success in entering a new market late is the exception, not the rule. All too often, successful companies hold the performance of small-market pioneers to the financial standards they apply to their own performance. In an attempt to ensure that they are using their resources well, companies explicitly or implicitly set relatively high thresholds for the size of the markets they should consider entering. This approach sentences them to making late entries into markets already filled with powerful players.

For example, when the 3.5-inch drive emerged, Seagate needed a $300-million-a-year product to replace its mature flagship 5.25-inch model, the ST412, and the 3.5-inch market wasn't large enough. Over the next two years, when the trade press asked when Seagate would introduce its 3.5-inch drive, company executives consistently responded that there was no market yet. There actually *was* a market, and it was growing rapidly. The signals that Seagate was picking up about the market, influenced as they were by customers who didn't want 3.5-inch drives, were misleading. When Seagate finally introduced its 3.5-inch drive in 1987, more than $750 million in 3.5-inch drives had already been sold. Information about the market's size had been widely available throughout the industry. But it wasn't compelling enough to shift the focus of Seagate's managers. They continued to look at the new market through the eyes of their current customers and in the context of their current financial structure.

The posture of today's leading disk-drive makers toward the newest disruptive technology, 1.8-inch drives, is eerily familiar. Each of the industry leaders has designed one or more models of the tiny drives, and the models are sitting on shelves. Their capacity is too low to be used in notebook computers, and no one yet knows where the initial market for 1.8-inch drives will be. Fax machines, printers, and automobile dashboard mapping systems are all candidates. "There just isn't a market," complained one industry executive. "We've got the product, and the sales force can take orders for it. But there are no orders because nobody needs it. It just sits there." This executive has not considered the fact that his sales force has no incentive to sell the

1.8-inch drives instead of the higher-margin products it sells to higher-volume customers. And while the 1.8-inch drive is sitting on the shelf at his company and others, last year more than $50 million worth of 1.8-inch drives were sold, almost all by start-ups. This year, the market will be an estimated $150 million.

To avoid allowing small, pioneering companies to dominate new markets, executives must personally monitor the available intelligence on the progress of pioneering companies through monthly meetings with technologists, academics, venture capitalists, and other nontraditional sources of information. They *cannot* rely on the company's traditional channels for gauging markets because those channels were not designed for that purpose.

Place Responsibility for Building a Disruptive-Technology Business in an Independent Organization

The strategy of forming small teams into skunk-works projects to isolate them from the stifling demands of mainstream organizations is widely known but poorly understood. For example, isolating a team of engineers so that it can develop a radically new sustaining technology just because that technology is radically different is a fundamental misapplication of the skunk-works approach. Managing out of context is also unnecessary in the unusual event that a disruptive technology is more financially attractive than existing products. Consider Intel's transition from dynamic random access memory (DRAM) chips to microprocessors. Intel's early microprocessor business had a higher gross margin than that of its DRAM business; in other words, Intel's normal resource-allocation process naturally provided the new business with the resources it needed.[1]

Creating a separate organization is necessary only when the disruptive technology has a lower profit margin than the mainstream business and must serve the unique needs of a new set of customers. CDC, for example, successfully created a remote organization to commercialize its 5.25-inch drive. Through 1980, CDC was the dominant independent disk-drive supplier due to its expertise in making 14-inch drives for mainframe-computer makers. When the 8-inch drive emerged, CDC launched a late development effort, but its engineers were repeatedly pulled off the project to solve problems for the more profitable, higher-priority 14-inch projects targeted at the company's most important customers. As a result, CDC was three years late in launching its first 8-inch product and never captured more than 5% of that market.

When the 5.25-inch generation arrived, CDC decided that it would face the new challenge more strategically. The company assigned a small group of engineers and marketers in Oklahoma City, Oklahoma, far from the mainstream organization's customers, the task of developing and commercializing a competitive 5.25-inch product. "We needed to launch it in an environment in which everybody got excited about a $50,000 order," one executive recalled. "In Minneapolis, you needed a $1 million order to turn anyone's head." CDC never regained the 70% share it had once enjoyed in the market for mainframe disk drives, but its Oklahoma

City operation secured a profitable 20% of the high-performance 5.25-inch market.

Had Apple created a similar organization to develop its Newton personal digital assistant (PDA), those who have pronounced it a flop might have deemed it a success. In launching the product, Apple made the mistake of acting as if it were dealing with an established market. Apple managers went into the PDA project assuming that it had to make a significant contribution to corporate growth. Accordingly, they researched customer desires exhaustively and then bet huge sums launching the Newton. Had Apple made a more modest technological and financial bet and entrusted the Newton to an organization the size that Apple itself was when it launched the Apple I, the outcome might have been different. The Newton might have been seen more broadly as a solid step forward in the quest to discover what customers really want. In fact, many more Newtons than Apple I models were sold within a year of their introduction.

Keep the Disruptive Organization Independent

Established companies can only dominate emerging markets by creating small organizations of the sort CDC created in Oklahoma City. But what should they do when the emerging market becomes large and established?

Most managers assume that once a spin-off has become commercially viable in a new market, it should be integrated into the mainstream organization. They reason that the fixed costs associated with engineering, manufacturing, sales, and distribution activities can be shared across a broader group of customers and products.

This approach might work with sustaining technologies; however, with disruptive technologies, folding the spin-off into the mainstream organization can be disastrous. When the independent and mainstream organizations are folded together in order to share resources, debilitating arguments inevitably arise over which groups get what resources and whether or when to cannibalize established products. In the history of the disk-drive industry, every company that has tried to manage main-stream and disruptive businesses within a single organization failed.

No matter the industry, a corporation consists of business units with finite life spans: the technological and market bases of any business will eventually disappear. Disruptive technologies are part of that cycle. Companies that understand this process can create new businesses to replace the ones that must inevitably die. To do so, companies must give managers of disruptive innovation free rein to realize the technology's full potential—even if it means ultimately killing the mainstream business. For the corporation to live, it must be willing to see business units die. If the corporation doesn't kill them off itself, competitors will.

The key to prospering at points of disruptive change is not simply to take more risks, invest for the long term, or fight bureaucracy. The key is to manage strategically important disruptive technologies in an organizational context where small orders create energy, where fast low-cost forays into ill-defined markets are possible, and where overhead is low enough to permit profit even in emerging markets.

Managers of established companies can master disruptive technologies with extraordinary success. But when they seek to develop and launch a disruptive technology that is rejected by important customers within the context of the mainstream business's financial demands, they fail—not because they make the wrong decisions, but because they make the right decisions for circumstances that are about to become history.

JOSEPH L. BOWER is the Donald Kirk David Professor of Business Administration at Harvard Business School. **CLAYTON M. CHRISTENSEN,** also a faculty member at Harvard Business School, specializes in managing the commercialization of advanced technology.

Note
1. Robert A. Burgelman, "Fading Memories: A Process Theory of Strategic Business Exit in Dynamic Environments," *Administrative Science Quarterly* 39 (1994), pp. 24–56.

Originally published in January 1995. Reprint 95103

Mapping Your Innovation Strategy

by Scott D. Anthony, Matt Eyring, and Lib Gibson

TO A CASUAL OBSERVER, American football seems pretty simple: You run, you pass, you kick, you pause an inordinate number of times for car commercials. However, any aficionado knows that football is, in reality, dizzyingly complex. A professional team's playbook looks about as thick as the Manhattan phone book. On any given down, the coach selects a formation and a specific play to run from that formation. All the players know their precise assignments for each play and how to adjust them if necessary.

Good coaches know the keys to winning consistently in ever changing circumstances. They need great playbooks that exploit the strengths of their rosters. They need to select plays on the basis of their opponents' strengths and weaknesses and the circumstances of each game. They must be prepared to adjust their game plans midstream. Players need to be flexible, too, ready to change on the fly in reaction to moves by their opponents. Teams that can accomplish these things, week after week of a grueling schedule, emerge as champions.

Most managers would grant that creating innovative growth businesses is at least as complicated as professional football. Yet all too many companies approach innovation without a game plan that positions them for success. Instead, they take the strategies that worked in the past and try to execute them better. Or they fumble in their search for markets that might welcome the technologies incubating in their labs. Ultimately, many companies come to some uneasy realizations: Their old plays are no longer effective. Their unsystematic efforts to create growth lead to random and often disappointing results. After repeated struggles, some managers throw their hands up and declare that bringing predictability to innovation is impossible. Indeed, there is a general sense that a fog enshrouds the world of innovation, obscuring high-potential opportunities and making success a hit-or-miss affair.

It doesn't have to be that way. Over the past five years, we've helped dozens of companies apply Harvard Business School professor Clayton Christensen's insights into disruptive innovation. Our work suggests that a few simple principles can help companies speed through the fuzzy front end of innovation. By creating a playbook for new growth, using it to identify the best opportunities, investing a little to learn a lot, and changing the corporate discourse, companies can develop a

Idea in Brief

Too many companies tackle new growth without a game plan. Instead, they reuse old growth strategies that worked in the past. Or they fumble to figure out markets that *might* welcome the technologies incubating in their labs. Consequently, the plays that worked so well previously are no longer effective. And hit-or-miss efforts to force new growth often spawn costly innovation failures.

Yet you *can* innovate better, faster, cheaper. How? Anthony, Eyring, and Gibson suggest these steps: Develop and execute an **innovation game plan.** Pick your playing field—**markets where the best opportunities are hiding and where you can play to your strengths.** Analyze major innovations in those markets to identify criteria your opportunity must meet to succeed. Develop a strategy for ensuring that your project meets those criteria. And fund the project conservatively at first, to force your innovation team to learn and adapt as it moves forward. Innovation won't ever be completely predictable. But play the game systematically, and you pull ahead of rivals still relying on trial and error to spur new growth. Your reward? Higher-quality innovations produced more quickly—with sharply lower investment.

process that produces high-quality innovations more quickly and with much less up-front investment.

Pick Your Playing Field

Before deciding *how* to play the innovation game, companies have to decide *where* to play. The good news is that, unlike professional sports teams that go where the schedule makers dictate, companies can choose to play in many different markets. But that is also the bad news. Too much choice can be overwhelming. And the innovation process can slow to a crawl if managers

Idea in Practice

To become an innovation champion, Anthony, Eyring, and Gibson recommend these steps.

Pick Your Playing Field

You face a bewildering array of possible markets for innovation. To narrow your choice, aim for markets lying somewhat out of—but not *too* far from—your core business. Find customers using existing products in unusual ways or using products for things they weren't designed to do. These behaviors signal the need for innovations.

Example: Software provider Intuit noticed that small business owners were using its *personal* financial software package because they liked its simplicity, compared to more complicated offerings designed for small businesses. Intuit optimized the program for these customers, branded it QuickBooks—and quickly dominated the product category.

Identify Success Criteria

Analyze major innovations in your targeted market's history to identify common elements shared by successful offerings.

Example: A consumer health care products company had identified at-home diagnostics as a key growth area. By analyzing the history of home diagnostics (pregnancy kits, blood glucose monitors), it identified eight characteristics shared by successful innovations. These included: diagnosing the condition is currently difficult, inconvenient, or expensive; competitors have difficulty duplicating the product; and the company could effectively communicate the innovation's benefits to target consumers.

Develop Your Own Innovation Game Plan

Assess your innovation opportunity against the

pursue opportunities that don't have a realistic chance of seeing the light of day.

One way to narrow down choices is to clarify what the company *won't* do. For example, a newspaper company that was looking into the wireless market set strict success criteria you identified. Brainstorm ideas for ensuring that the opportunity meets the criteria.

> **Example:** Procter & Gamble wanted to bring a leading brand to China. Success criteria included low cost but "good enough" performance. Yet stripping out functionality to lower costs would annoy demanding consumers—*not* a criterion for success. P&G's plan? Start in smaller Chinese cities, where consumers would embrace limited first-generation products because no legitimate alternatives existed. After resolving the inevitable kinks in producing such a low-cost product and improving quality, P&G would take the offering to larger cities.

Execute and Adapt

All innovations unfold in unpredictable ways. To boost your chances of success, follow the principle "Invest a little, learn a lot."

> **Example:** Teradyne, a semiconductor test equipment maker, saw an opportunity to create smaller, cheaper, and easier-to-use machines. The CEO demanded that the innovation team achieve early profitability before he invested significantly in the project. This requirement forced the team to find a foothold market they could attack quickly: manufacturers who produced inexpensive commodity semiconductors that perform basic computations in household appliances. These manufacturers—who couldn't previously afford Teradyne's offerings—loved the new product. It took off, creating a substantial growth business for Teradyne.

boundaries: no gaming, no gambling, and no personal ads. The company knew those boundaries left promising growth opportunities on the table, but they also kept middle managers from wasting time on ideas that senior managers would ultimately kill.

The Disruptive Playbook

AT THE CORE OF THE DISRUPTIVE innovation theory developed by Harvard Business School professor Clayton Christensen is a simple principle: Companies innovate faster than people's lives change. Most organizations make products that are too good, too expensive, and too inconvenient for many customers. This happens for a good reason. After all, managers are trained to seek higher profits by bringing better products to the most demanding customers. But in the pursuit of profits, companies overshoot less-demanding customers who are perfectly willing to take the basics at reasonable prices. And they ignore nonconsumers who may need to get a job done but lack the skills, wealth, or ability to adopt existing solutions.

Companies seeking to create growth through disruption can run three basic plays, each of which is suited to certain circumstances.

The Back-Scratcher: Scratch an Unscratched Itch

What it is: Make it easier and simpler for people to get an important job done.

When it works best: When customers are frustrated by their inability to get a job done and competitors are either fragmented or have a disability that prevents them from responding.

Historical examples: Federal Express, Intuit's QuickBooks.

Current examples: Procter & Gamble's Swiffer products, instant messaging technology.

Paradoxically, these kinds of constraints can be liberating, helping to focus managers' creative energy. The search for new growth, however, can still be daunting. Most companies intuitively sense that the best place to look for growth is outside of—but not too far from—their

The Extreme Makeover: Make an Ugly Business Attractive

What it is: Find a way to prosper at the low end of established markets by giving people good enough solutions at low prices.

When it works best: When target customers don't need and don't value all the performance that can be packed into products and when existing competitors don't focus on low-end customers.

Historical examples: Nucor's steel mini-mill, Toyota Corona.

Current examples: India-based Tata's sub-$3,000 automobile, exchange-traded mutual funds.

The Bottleneck Buster: Democratize a Limited Market

What it is: Expand a market by removing a barrier to consumption.

When it works best: When some customers are locked out of a market because they lack skills, access, or wealth. Competitors ignore initial developments because they take place in seemingly unpromising markets.

Historical examples: Personal computers, balloon angioplasty, Sony Walkman, eBay.

Current examples: Blogs, home diagnostics.

---

core business. But where? We believe that strategies based on disruptive innovations have the highest chances of creating growth. Generally speaking, these innovations offer lower performance along dimensions that incumbent firms consider critical. In exchange, they introduce benefits such as simplicity, convenience, ease of use, and low prices. To spot markets that have a high potential for a disruptive approach, we ask three basic questions. (For a closer look at the three questions, see the sidebar "The Disruptive Playbook.")

What jobs can't our existing customers get done?
As Christensen has pointed out, when customers buy products, they are in essence hiring them to get important jobs done. Companies can start the search for growth opportunities by examining why customers hire their current products. That understanding can point to related jobs that customers can't get done.

Consider how software provider Intuit developed the insight that led to its massively successful QuickBooks package. In the early 1990s, Intuit observed that many people who used Quicken, the company's personal financial software, were small-business owners. That was curious because Intuit hadn't designed the software to manage a business. The company realized that the job these customers had to get done was a simple one: Make sure I don't run out of cash. Software programs such as Peachtree that were designed for the small-business market were generally packed with complicated functions like depreciation schedules, which small-business owners found unnecessary and intimidating. Intuit realized that users enjoyed Quicken's simplicity and easy-to-navigate user interface. Intuit adapted that program for small-business owners, branded it under the QuickBooks name, and quickly became the dominant player in the category. "We uncovered a giant opportunity," Intuit cofounder Scott Cook said. "The majority of small-business people do not have the skill to utilize debit- and credit-based software, but they have to keep books."

As the Intuit example shows, it's important to notice if your customers are using existing products in unusual ways, stretching them to do something they were not designed for, or "kludging" several together for a suboptimal solution. Those compensating behaviors signal that customers do not have access to the ideal product. None of the solutions small-business owners hired for the "don't run out of cash" job—pen and paper, Quicken, Excel spreadsheets—were a perfect fit, which spelled opportunity for innovation.

Who are the industry's worst customers?

An industry's worst customers might sound like the last place to look for new growth. But thinking about ways to serve seemingly undesirable customers can point to novel strategies. Global silicone leader Dow Corning, for example, found a successful growth strategy by focusing on the low end of its customer base. The company produces the world's highest-quality silicones, used in applications ranging from shampoos to space shuttles. Dow Corning's scientists provide high value-added services to its customers. Yet the company found that its traditional business model actually overshot the needs of customers looking for basic silicones at reasonable prices. Those seemingly unattractive customers were turning to low-cost competitors that provided less-advanced products and no-frills service.

As the industry's largest player, Dow Corning would be able to take advantage of scale economics to play in this tier of the market—if it could reconstitute its business model. In 2002, it launched a distribution channel called Xiameter, designed to compete at the commodity end of the silicone business. By embracing a business model that differs sharply from its core model, Dow Corning is prospering in a very challenging market space.

Where are there barriers that constrain consumption?
Throughout history, some of the most powerful growth strategies have democratized markets, blowing open select groups of the few, the trained, and the wealthy and thereby dramatically expanding consumption. Companies should scan for markets limited in various ways. Sometimes markets are constrained because products are too expensive for mass consumption. Sometimes the need for expertise limits a market to those with special training. Sometimes the need to go to a centralized setting, such as having to go to a doctor's office for a diagnosis, makes it difficult for individuals who prefer to "do it themselves."

Looking for such pools of bottled-up consumption led Turner Broadcasting System, a multibillion-dollar subsidiary of Time Warner, to a counterintuitive growth strategy. All of Turner's successes had been cable channels, like Cable News Network (CNN), Turner Classic Movies (TCM), and the Cartoon Network. In each case, the company had succeeded by obtaining basic content at a reasonable price and then shaping and molding it into a differentiated offering.

To find new growth, Turner looked for nontelevision markets that might have desirable content consumers couldn't easily access. The search led to gaming. Gaming companies had vast stores of content they pulled off the shelves years ago, just like the old movies that air on TCM. A consumer looking for one of those games had to put up with inferior online replications or try to find the original game on eBay—and that option would work only if the consumer owned the console on which the game operated.

Turner's strategy attempted to expand consumption of out-of-circulation games. The company licensed thousands of games—from timeless classics like Pong and Asteroids to more recent hits like Tomb Raider and Splinter Cell—and in 2005 launched a Web-based subscription service called GameTap. Although it is too early to measure results, the company's approach is consistent with other democratizing innovations that have created substantial growth businesses.

Build Your Growth Playbook

Once a company has identified the market space it wishes to target, it's time to look more specifically at how to serve that market. As an example, consider MinuteClinic, an emerging provider of health care diagnostic services. Its kiosks, located in stores such as Target and CVS, offer a menu of services for diagnosing about 25 straightforward ailments, including strep throat and pinkeye. The nurse practitioner who staffs the kiosk can reliably diagnose the conditions in less than 15 minutes and write a prescription that the customer can fill in the in-store pharmacy.

MinuteClinic shares the following characteristics with other disruptive innovations:

- **The target customer is looking for something different because existing solutions are too expensive, too complicated, or don't quite get the job done.** Minute-Clinic's customers aren't looking for better-trained doctors; they are looking for speed and convenience.

- **The solution is good enough along traditional performance dimensions and superior along other dimensions that matter more to target customers.** MinuteClinic can't treat everything. If a customer comes in and says, "I feel dizzy" or "Something is wrong with me, but I don't know what," MinuteClinic refers the patient to a physician in a traditional setting. But MinuteClinic has better performance along dimensions its customers care about—speed and convenience.

- **The business model has low overhead and high asset utilization, allowing companies to offer low prices or serve small markets.** MinuteClinic, with its lean overhead and effective software systems, can provide a lower-cost solution that is extremely appealing to insurers and corporate sponsors.

- **The strategy is not one that powerful incumbents initially want to pursue themselves.** Many primary care physicians welcome MinuteClinic's solution because it frees them to work on the more complicated problems that are a better fit with their training.

While this basic disruptive pattern holds true across industries, companies need to customize an approach that reflects the idiosyncrasies of their particular markets. Thus they need to develop checklists that spell out the market circumstances where the approach has the best chance of succeeding and identify criteria to which successful strategies should conform.

One way to develop such a checklist is to analyze ten to 15 major innovations in the market segment's history. Look at both successes and failures, particularly the "sure-fire" strategies that flopped and the "unpromising" ones that were runaway successes. Figure out the elements shared by the truly successful strategies. Combine the results of this historical analysis with the basic disruptive principles, and you have your customized checklist, or playbook. For example, a consumer health care company identified at-home diagnostics as a key growth area. It was interested in understanding why some consumer-based diagnostics, such as pregnancy kits and blood glucose monitors, took off while others, like home drug tests, floundered. By analyzing the history of home diagnostics from a disruptive perspective, the company identified the characteristics shared by successful innovations. It then created a 20-point checklist to assess new products that included elements such as the following:

- Is the diagnostic job important to the consumer?

- Is diagnosing currently very difficult, inconvenient, or expensive?

- Are results conclusive without further testing or triaging of symptoms?

- Is the diagnostic linked to treatment or follow-up action?

- Are we capable of developing the necessary technology?

- Can we communicate effectively to the target consumer?

- Will influencers (such as professional caregivers and insurers) actively support the diagnostic?

- Will our competitors have difficulty duplicating this product?

The checklist allowed the company to look at any opportunity from multiple perspectives, including those of consumers, competitors, the channel, and regulators. The diversity of perspectives allowed the company to avoid a classic trap: a myopic focus on innovation within a company's comfort zone. For example, a firm with a strong engineering culture might focus primarily on whether it can solve a tough technological problem. This kind of focused question is important, but companies that don't also develop a holistic sense of an opportunity run the risk of missing important elements that can come back to bite them.

With these guidelines in hand, companies can then begin to move from generic plays to specific opportunities for innovation.

Build Your Innovation Game Plan

Now it's time to create a short list of innovation ideas for your target market and to assess whether those ideas adhere to the general pattern of success you've uncovered and to your specific checklist.

The discipline of checking seemingly high-potential ideas against a rigorous list of questions should keep you from moving forward with a plan that's similar to something that worked in the past but different in some crucial way. For example, Procter & Gamble has time and again leveraged its massive distribution power to muscle itself into a product category. To take just one example, in 1999 the consumer products giant purchased Iams, a niche pet food provider, for $2.3 billion. By improving an already good product and bringing it to tens of thousands of grocery stores, where it competed against fragmented providers, P&G created a blockbuster brand. However, when P&G tried to enter the prepackaged cookie market with its Duncan Hines soft-baked cookies in the 1980s, it was a different story. The market was not fragmented, and strong competitors Keebler and Nabisco reacted ferociously to P&G's entry. Although P&G claimed the rivals had infringed its patents (and ultimately won a lawsuit), it had to exit the market. P&G's classic consolidation-and-distribution play worked when competitors were fragmented but failed when two powerful incumbents were among them. A checklist that included questions about the clout of potential competitors might have alerted managers to the problem.

Creating Specific Opportunities

Let's look in detail at how one company identified, then assessed, a potential innovation. Ethicon Endo-Surgery, a multibillion-dollar company, sells equipment for minimally invasive surgeries. In analyzing the industry's pattern of success, EES managers realized that the most successful new medical devices typically enabled less highly trained (and less costly) practitioners to treat patients themselves instead of referring them to specialists.

EES managers then looked methodically for an existing surgical procedure characterized by a lot of seemingly avoidable high costs. They learned that more than a quarter of colon resections—painful, invasive, high-cost procedures—remove a benign growth. That figure seemed high, so EES managers started talking to leading gastroenterologists, many of whom had a rule of thumb: Any growth of more than two centimeters gets referred to a surgeon because the gastroenterologist can't efficiently remove such polyps, which are often cancerous. Once EES identified this circumstance, which had high potential for a novel approach, it started looking for a specific technology to bring to the market. Some internal brainstorming, followed by an intensive survey of external technologies and development work, led to a project to develop a device that would enable gastroenterologists or clinicians to remove large polyps noninvasively, during a colonoscopy. Clinicians who have used the device say that it has the potential to become the new standard of care, allowing more practitioners to treat patients less invasively and in less centralized settings.

The process of assessing an opportunity against a checklist often leads a company to go ahead with the project—but adjust it in some crucial way to fit the pattern of successful innovations. For example, a team at P&G was evaluating a strategy to bring one of its leading brands to China. The team knew its solution had to be very low cost and still perform adequately along dimensions that consumers cared about. But to get the product to a low enough price point, P&G would need to strip out functionality that demanding consumers in the country's largest cities considered critical. This assessment led P&G to start in smaller Chinese cities, where consumers for whom existing alternatives were too expensive would embrace P&G's limited first-generation product. As P&G works out the inevitable kinks in manufacturing such a low-cost product and improves its functionality, it plans to introduce the product in larger cities.

Focusing on Patterns Instead of Numbers

Many seasoned innovators might be asking themselves, "But what about the numbers?" Obviously, when you're planning to launch a product or service, you can't ignore financial data. However, our experience suggests that most companies force teams to develop detailed financial estimates way too early, when their accuracy will necessarily be low. Using metrics such as net present value (NPV) or return on investment (ROI) as rough guidelines is fine. Using them as rank-ordering tools to make decisions is counterproductive.

Here's why: Companies that rank projects using detailed financial metrics won't end up selecting ones aimed at the seemingly small, difficult-to-measure markets that are so often the footholds for powerful growth strategies. Instead, they'll likely move forward with projects in large, measurable markets—the ones that are usually hostile to disruptive innovations. As a result, new products often fail to deliver significant, differentiated new benefits, or the company suffers a devastating response from incumbents.

Instead of fretting over precise figures, play the "number of zeros" game. Determine whether the revenue created by an opportunity will have eight zeros on the end ($100 million) or five ($100,000). Focusing on the assumptions behind those estimates—what must be true for those estimates to be plausible—is meaningful. Arguing about whether an opportunity will produce revenues of $23 million or $28 million is pointless at this early stage.

Detailed metrics make sense for product extensions in known markets. Innovation strategies that are markedly different need an appropriately different evaluation process. A company's early focus has to be on how well the innovation fits with the pattern of success. Had the P&G team mentioned earlier focused on detailed metrics too soon, it probably would have decided to start in China's largest cities. After all, that approach would appear to yield the highest first-year sales and NPV figures. By paying attention to its playbook, however, the team saw that starting in the big cities would actually lead to failure.

Execute and Adapt

If everything went exactly as coaches diagrammed, football would be a pretty boring game (rugby fans might argue that it already is pretty boring). The result of any play would be perfectly predictable. In reality, however, plays often unfold in completely unanticipated ways. Companies need to make sure that as they begin to execute their new-growth game plans, they, too, encourage adaptation and flexibility. They can do this by following a simple mantra: Invest a little, learn a lot.

Big companies often think their deeper pockets give them an advantage over start-ups. But sometimes extra financing is a curse. Project teams with too much money may keep going in the wrong direction for too long. Those with scarce resources, however, must scramble to find novel approaches that they might not otherwise discover.

One powerful example of this principle is Teradyne's efforts in the late 1990s to create a disruptive product in semiconductor test equipment. Teradyne's CEO at the time, Alex d'Arbeloff, recognized that emerging technologies would allow the company to create machines that were dramatically smaller, cheaper, and simpler to use than the products it currently sold to market leaders like Intel. The new machines wouldn't be as functional, but they might be good enough for some market segments. It felt like a classic case of disruptive innovation.

D'Arbeloff gave the team, code-named Aurora, modest revenue expectations—$1 million in year one and $11 million in year two—but demanded that it achieve profitability before he invested significant sums of money. By constraining the team's financial (and therefore engineering) resources, he forced it to find a foothold market it could attack quickly. The team just didn't have the luxury of spending years in development to make the product good enough for Teradyne's core customers. Although team members occasionally muttered not-so-nice things under their breath about d'Arbeloff, scarcity compelled them to experiment with novel approaches. Ultimately, the team found a surprising way into the market by targeting manufacturers who produced inexpensive commodity semiconductors that perform basic computations in household appliances such as toasters. Historically, these customers couldn't afford Teradyne's expensive, complicated test equipment, but they loved the simpler, cheaper Aurora product. The product took off and created a substantial growth business for Teradyne.

Some managers might be nodding their heads at this point, thinking, "We get this. We have brought the venture capital approach into our organization." Our experience suggests that many companies that think they are following an "invest a little, learn a lot" approach are actually falling into one of three classic traps: They are unwilling to kill projects that have fatal flaws; they commit too much capital too soon, allowing a project team to follow the wrong approach for too long; or they fail to adapt their strategies even in the face of information that suggests their current approach is wrong.

To avoid these mistakes, companies should be rigorous about staging their investments. Early investments should focus on resolving critical unknowns. Identifying where the team should focus is straightforward. Just ask the following questions: What is the consequence of being wrong about an assumption? Is it catastrophic or potentially harmless? How much certainty do I have that I am right? Enough to bet my job on it? How long would it take and how much would it cost to become more knowledgeable?

By answering these questions and identifying critical assumptions, teams can direct their investments to the appropriate experiments. After running the experiments, companies then have one of four options:

- **Double down:** Information clearly points to a winning strategy with no obvious deal-killing uncertainties, so move forward rapidly.

- **Continue exploring:** All signs look positive, but there are still untested assumptions, so keep experimenting.

- **Adjust the game plan:** Investigation suggests that the current strategy is not viable, but another approach might be, so change the approach and begin experimenting again.

- **Shelve:** There is no clear path forward, so move on to other projects until something else changes.

The key is to make decisions rapidly. We have seen companies seeking to build their innovation capabilities try to move dozens of ideas forward simultaneously. Starting with a lot of ideas is important, but success requires the fortitude to shut down the unpromising ones and redirect those that are heading in the wrong direction. If companies wait too long to make these decisions, they end up diverting resources toward fruitless efforts or continuing to execute a fatally flawed strategy. Consider the words of a newspaper editor who faced this difficulty as his company attempted to innovate on the Internet: "Given the pace of our expansion, I don't think we made mistakes fast enough, and we didn't learn from them often enough. The problem wasn't just turning [the experiments] on, sometimes it was turning them off."

Change Your Role

It will come as no surprise that senior management has an important role to play in building a strong capability around growth and innovation. Creating a separate pool of resources for growth initiatives and fiercely protecting that pool is one obvious step. But senior managers need to do more than provide resources. They need to shield innovation projects as if they were viruses threatened by corporate antibodies. And they need to work with innovators to solve vexing strategic issues.

Blocking the Antibodies

Consider a chemical company that was working with a wide array of suppliers to quickly bring customized products to the marketplace. The strategy was very different from the one the company used in its core business, where it worked with just a few suppliers and followed a very rigorous and lengthy process to ensure that suppliers met high quality standards. That process worked extremely well when the company was adding another core supplier. However, it crippled the new approach, which focused on mix-and-match, fast customization. By the time a supplier received clearance, a window of opportunity had slammed shut.

With this realization, senior management gave the team "process FastPass" cards modeled on Disney's program that allows people to cut to the front of lines on popular rides. As long as the team had convincing evidence that using a supplier would not get the company in trouble, it could bypass the standard approval process. Fortunately, most of the suppliers in question worked with other industry players and so easily passed that litmus test.

Mobile phone giant Motorola applied a similar principle while developing its ultra-thin Razr phone. Usually, when Motorola planned to develop a new phone, representatives from each of the company's major geographic regions (Europe, Asia, and so on) weighed in on the concept. The regions would request the sorts of features and functions they wanted in the design. Each region would then forecast how many units of the model it thought would sell. The aggregated regional plans would help Motorola decide whether to invest in the phone.

It was always a complicated dance. If a development team ignored features that a specific region deemed critical, that region would project low sales, which would make it tougher for the development team to get approval for the project. Teams knew, then, that they had to appease each of the regions. Although this system ensured that products reflected some critical feedback from the regions, it could force designers to develop compromise products that were acceptable to everyone yet delightful to no one.

With the Razr, Motorola's management sensed an opportunity to buck industry trends. Whereas competitors were racing to cram more features and functionality onto handsets, Motorola decided to limit features and focus on form, creating the smallest, thinnest phone on the market. Luckily, management recognized that it had to buffer the Razr team if it wanted to introduce this blockbuster innovation. Senior management exempted the Razr from the company's standard development process, giving the team freedom to create a novel product that delighted customers and caught competitors off guard. The Razr exceeded the company's total lifetime projections for the product in its first three months, turning into a massive success story for Motorola.

Changing the Conversation
In addition to shielding project teams, senior managers must also change the discourse with them. As more and more companies have adopted stage-gate processes to

manage innovation, an us-against-them mentality has emerged. Teams present to senior managers, who then act as gatekeepers, either opening the gate to let projects through or locking it until the team comes back with better numbers or more proof. When the right strategy is unknown and unknowable—as it so often is with novel growth initiatives—senior managers need to be problem solvers, not dictators.

Karl Ronn from P&G embodies this notion. Ronn, the vice president for research and development for the company's home care division, oversees such brands as Mr. Clean, Dawn, Swiffer, and Febreze. When a team is working on an incremental line extension, Ronn receives results at predetermined milestones. But when P&G is developing extremely novel products, such as the Mr. Clean Magic Eraser or Flick (a version of Swiffer that cleans carpets), Ronn acts differently. Instead of reviewing results of agreed-upon decisions, he and the business unit president go into the labs to review early prototypes and participate in daylong brainstorming sessions. Such deeper engagement allows senior managers to get a better feel for the new products and share their collective wisdom with the team. "This is not like a Skunk Works where we cut out the middle managers," Ronn said. "Rather, we are there with them to help and also to learn about the business before we have to invest in it."

Generally, senior managers overseeing novel growth strategies need to engage frequently with the managers developing and implementing them. Quarterly meetings either slow progress or lead teams to make critical decisions without senior management's guidance.

Changing the Innovation Mind-Set

IMPLEMENTING THE PRINCIPLES we discuss can allow companies to embrace new innovation mind-sets:

- **Good enough can be great.** Many companies unintentionally slow the innovation process by pushing for perfection. eBay CEO Meg Whitman, quoted in a March 2005 issue of *USA Today,* put in nicely: "It's better to put something out there and see the reaction and fix it on the fly ... It's another way of saying 'perfect' is the enemy of 'good enough.'"

- **Step, don't leap.** Great leaps forward, when companies spend many years and millions of dollars seeking to jump over existing companies, almost never work. Companies have a much greater chance of success if they start with a simple springboard. Think about the journey of P&G's Febreze brand. P&G initially positioned Febreze as a "removing odor" brand by packaging it to look like other household cleaners and placing it in the laundry aisle next to such powerhouse brands as Tide and Downy. The company then introduced Air Effects, thus moving Febreze toward a "clean the air" brand. In early 2006 P&G introduced Febreze Noticeables, a plug-in air freshener that alternates between two scents. P&G has obviously moved squarely into the air freshening market, but it has done so in a thoughtful, staged way.

- **The right kind of failure is success.** Most well-run companies naturally consider failure to be highly undesirable. But remember, most of the time the initial strategy for a growth business is going to be wrong. Managers need to recognize that learning what's wrong with an approach and adapting appropriately is a good thing, not a failure. The Mayo Clinic gives a "queasy eagle" award to individuals who fail for the right reason. Managers must balance the confidence to start going in an uncertain direction, the humility to recognize that the direction is wrong, and the fortitude to listen, learn, and adapt.

Now, of course senior management can't be deeply engaged in every project. If a project is in a well-known market, it's appropriate for senior management to act as a traditional gatekeeper. Nor should senior managers abdicate their role as decision makers who determine when a team has learned enough to continue moving forward. But if neither management nor the team knows the answer, senior managers ought to break out of the us-versus-them mind-set and use their strategic thinking skills to help the team solve problems. (See the sidebar "Changing the Innovation Mind-Set" for other important changes.)

Companies can pierce the fog of innovation. An unpredictable innovation process teeming with trade-offs between speed, quality, and investment can become better, faster, and cheaper. By allocating resources more efficiently and accelerating the highest-potential innovations, companies can enjoy a winning streak of innovation successes that will throw competitors off balance.

But the opportunity that now exists to build a competitive advantage through innovation won't last forever. That's because problem-solving approaches evolve in a predictable way. When people first encounter a new type of challenge, they must solve it using an unstructured, trial-and-error approach. Over time, as they learn more about that particular challenge, clear rules emerge to guide problem-solving efforts. We believe that innovation is now somewhere between random trial-and-error and perfectly predictable, paint-by-number rules. We think of this transitional period as the era of pattern recognition, during which companies can create competitive advantage by becoming world-class at defining and executing against patterns. As the patterns we've identified become more obvious—and as others emerge—it will once again become difficult to base a sustainable competitive advantage on innovation competencies. But for the moment, forward-thinking companies can head out in new directions by learning how to see patterns where others see chaos.

SCOTT D. ANTHONY is the managing director of Innosight, a consulting firm in Massachusetts, and a coauthor of *Seeing What's Next* (Harvard Business Review Press, 2004). **MATT EYRING** is the managing director of Innosight Capital. **LIB GIBSON** is a corporate adviser in the office of the CEO at Bell Canada Enterprises.

Originally published in May 2006. Reprint R0605F

Index

You don't want to miss these...

We've combed through hundreds of *Harvard Business Review* articles on key management topics and selected *the* most important ones to help you maximize your own and your organization's performance.

10 Must-Read Articles on:

LEADERSHIP
How can you transform yourself from a good manager into an extraordinary leader?

STRATEGY
Is your company spending an enormous amount of time and energy on strategy development, with little to show for its efforts?

MANAGING YOURSELF
The path to your own professional success starts with a critical look in the mirror.

CHANGE
70 percent of all change initiatives fail. Learn how to turn the odds in your company's favor.

MANAGING PEOPLE
What really motivates people? How do you deal with problem employees? How can you build a team that is greater than the sum of its parts?

THE ESSENTIALS
If you read nothing else, read these 10 articles from some of *Harvard Business Review*'s most influential authors.

Harvard Business Review Press

Yours for only $24.95 each.
10 articles in each collection.
Available in PDF or paperback.

Order online at mustreads.hbr.org
or call us at 800-668-6780.
Outside the U.S. and Canada,
call +1 617-783-7450.